C. RHODES

# ELFEZ
## THE UNDOCUMENTED ELF THAT SAVED CHRISTMAS

**TEXT: BEE SACRAMENTO**
**ILLUSTRATION: KRISTIN CARELLA**

© The Cal Rhodes Cartoon Company

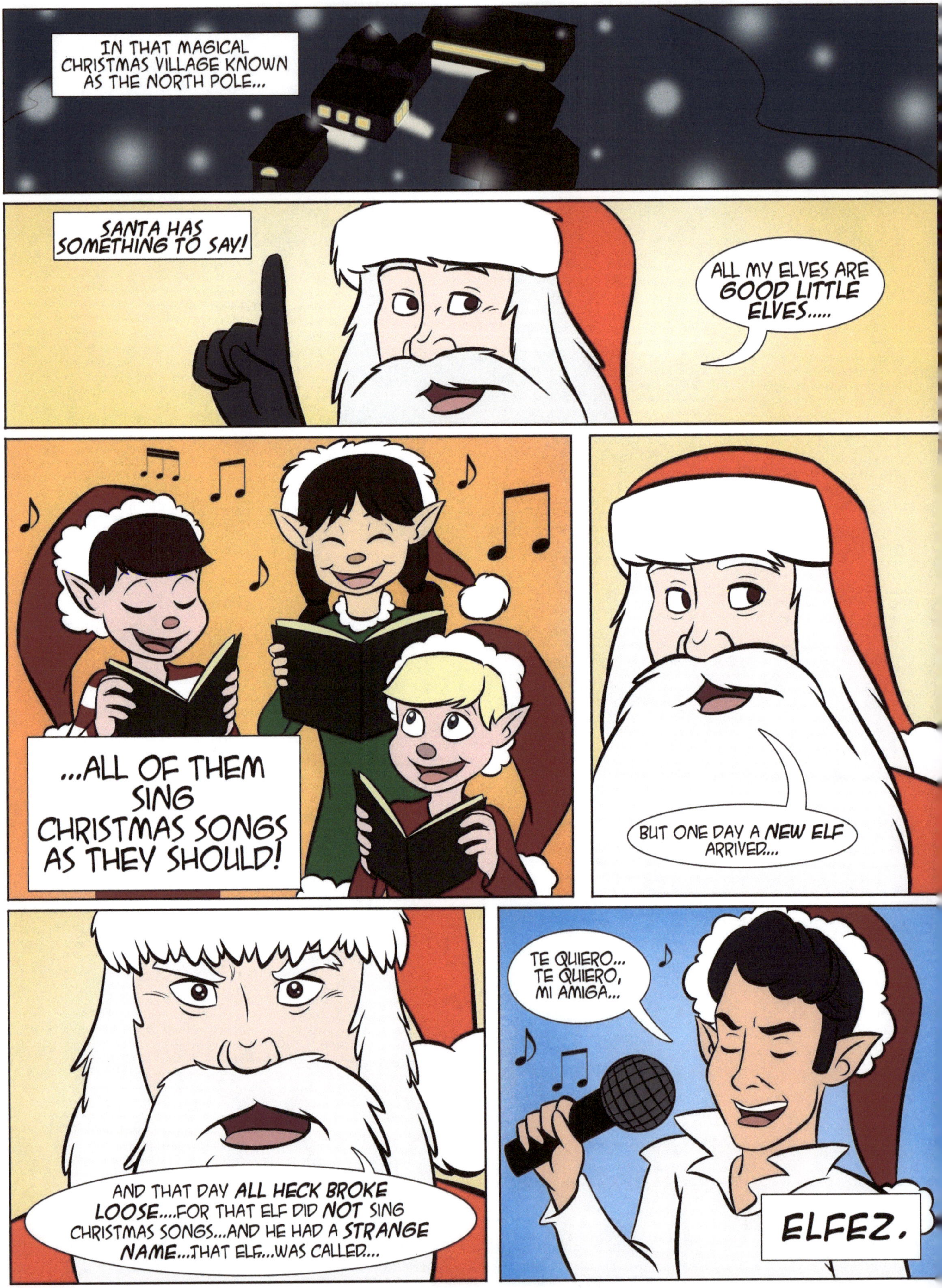
IN THAT MAGICAL CHRISTMAS VILLAGE KNOWN AS THE NORTH POLE...
SANTA HAS SOMETHING TO SAY!
ALL MY ELVES ARE GOOD LITTLE ELVES.....
...ALL OF THEM SING CHRISTMAS SONGS AS THEY SHOULD!
BUT ONE DAY A NEW ELF ARRIVED....
AND THAT DAY ALL HECK BROKE LOOSE....FOR THAT ELF DID NOT SING CHRISTMAS SONGS...AND HE HAD A STRANGE NAME....THAT ELF...WAS CALLED....
TE QUIERO... TE QUIERO, MI AMIGA...
ELFEZ.

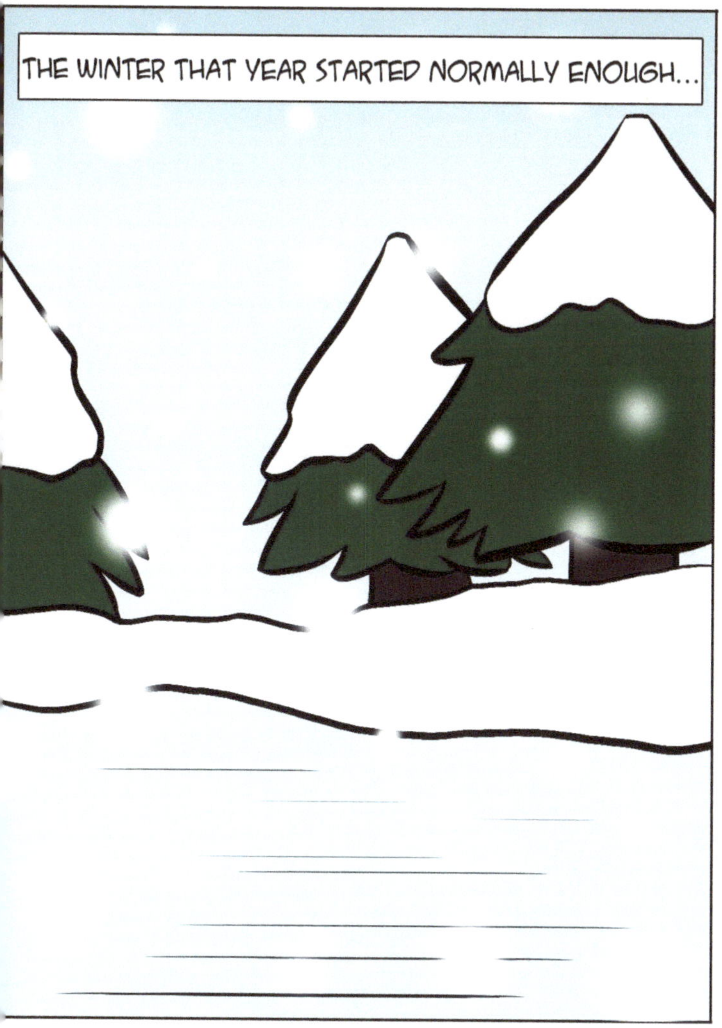
THE WINTER THAT YEAR STARTED NORMALLY ENOUGH...

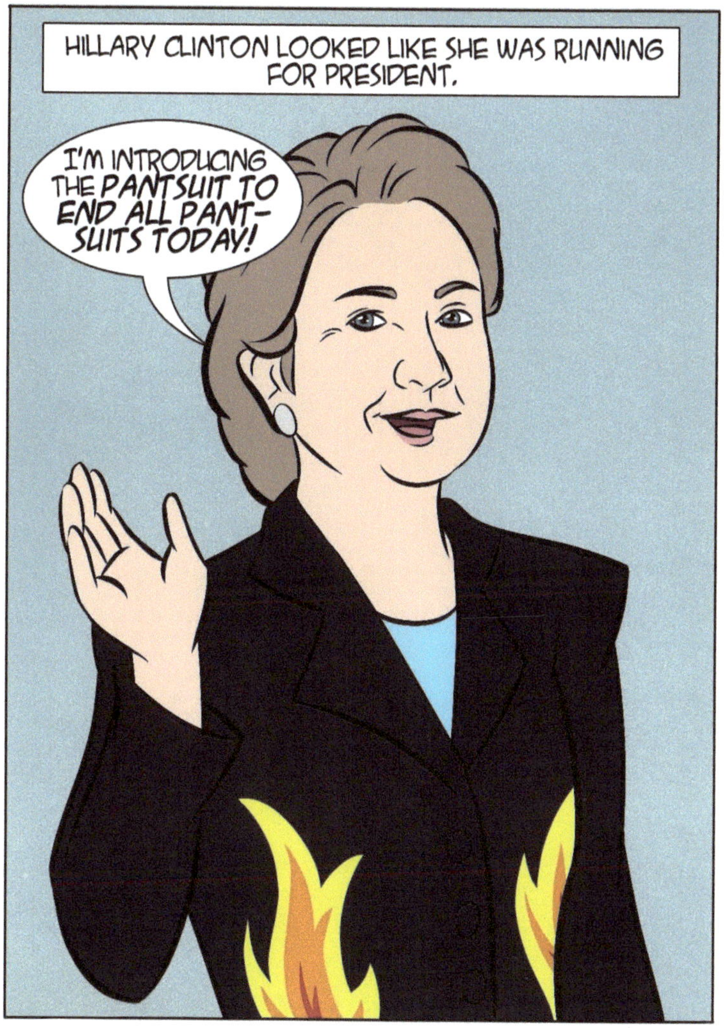
HILLARY CLINTON LOOKED LIKE SHE WAS RUNNING FOR PRESIDENT.
I'M INTRODUCING THE PANTSUIT TO END ALL PANT-SUITS TODAY!

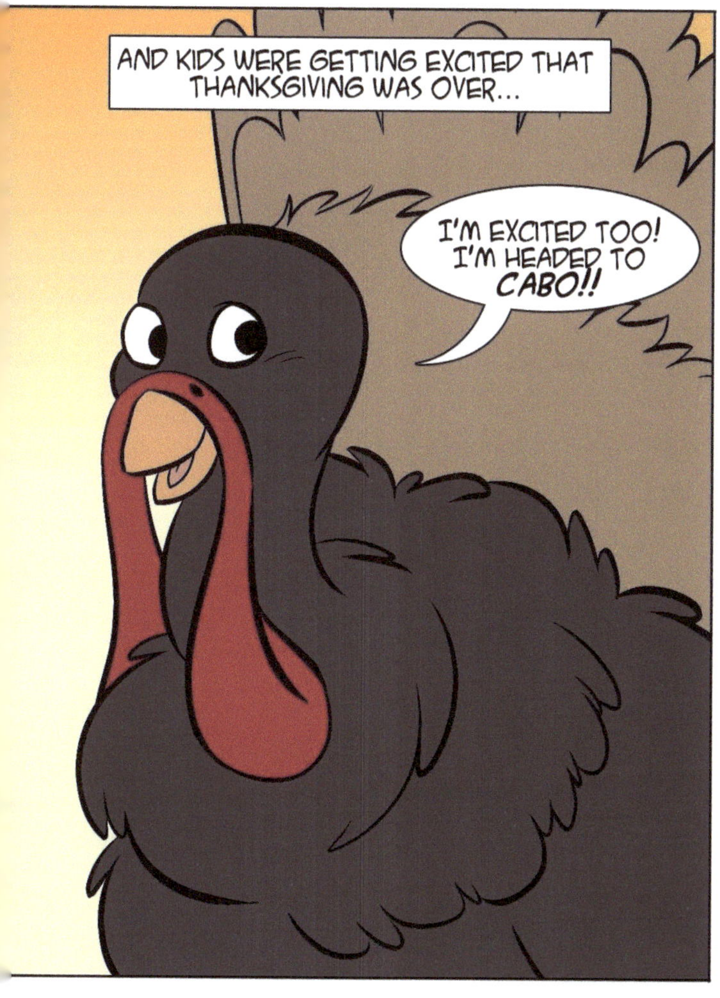
AND KIDS WERE GETTING EXCITED THAT THANKSGIVING WAS OVER...
I'M EXCITED TOO! I'M HEADED TO CABO!!

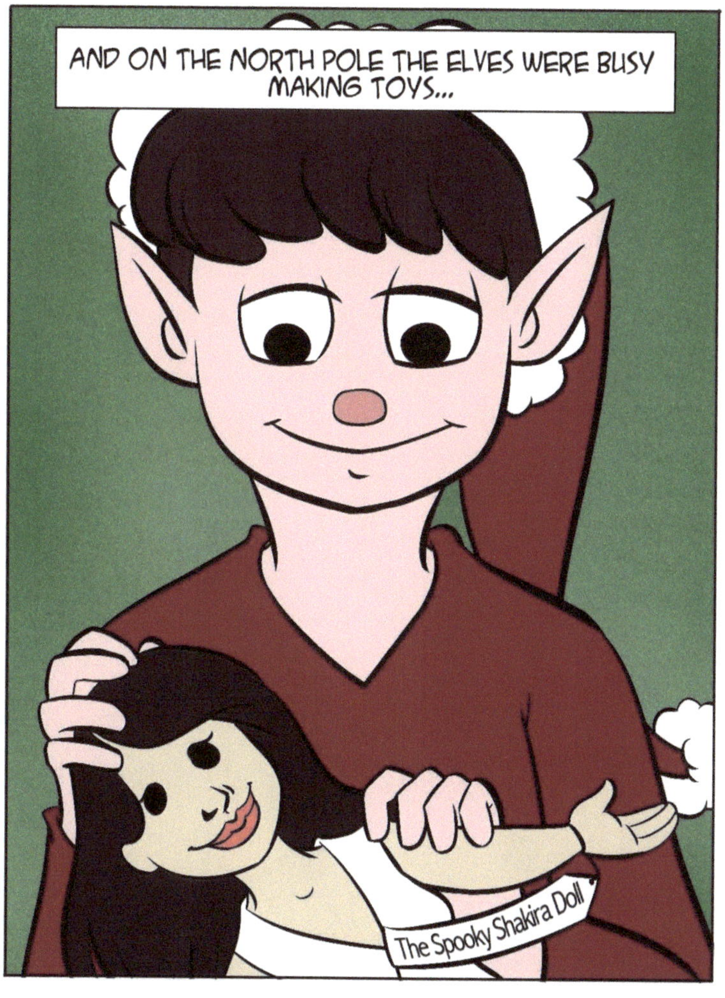
AND ON THE NORTH POLE THE ELVES WERE BUSY MAKING TOYS...
The Spooky Shakira Doll

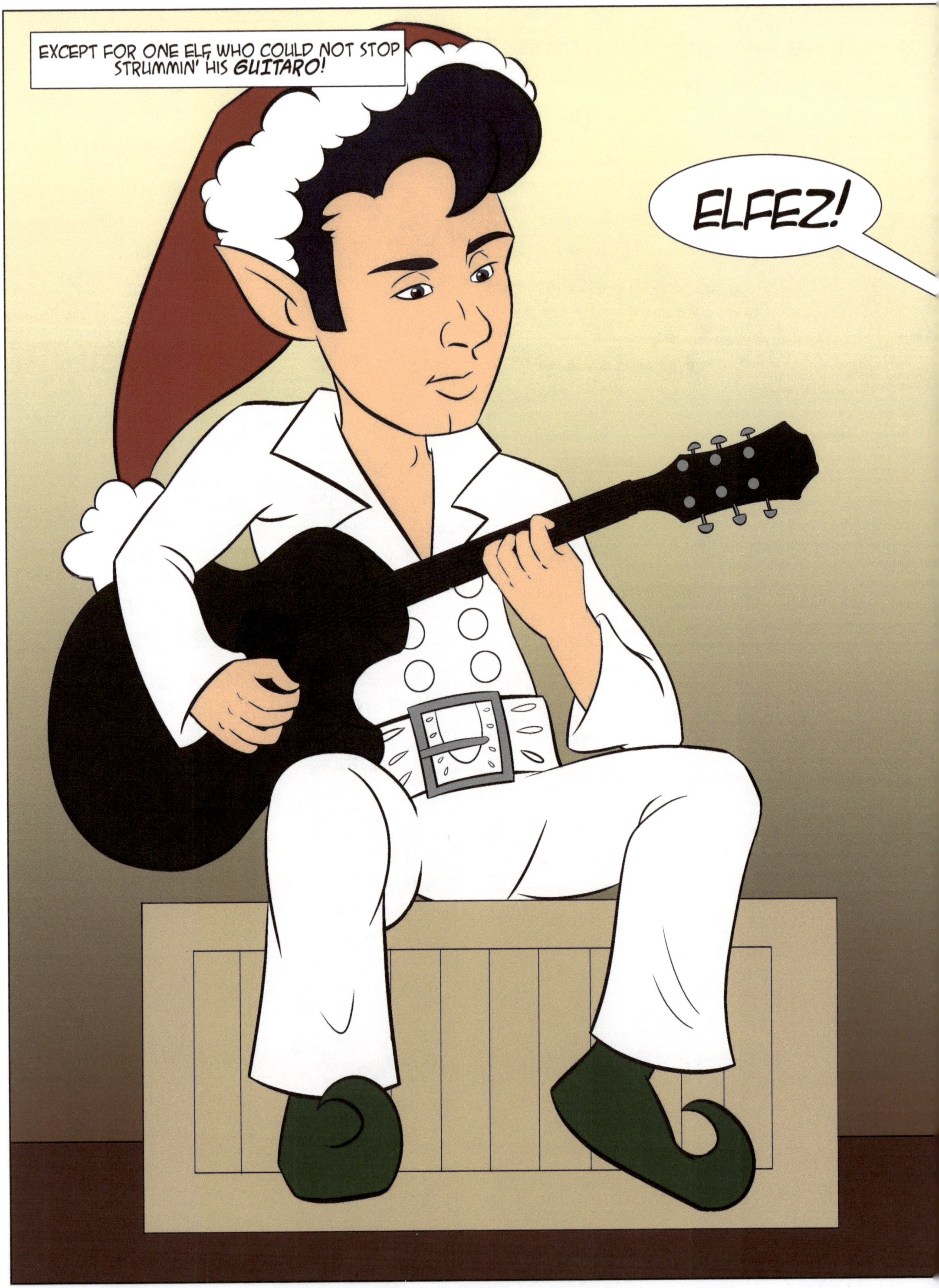
EXCEPT FOR ONE ELF WHO COULD NOT STOP STRUMMIN' HIS GUITARO!
ELFEZ!

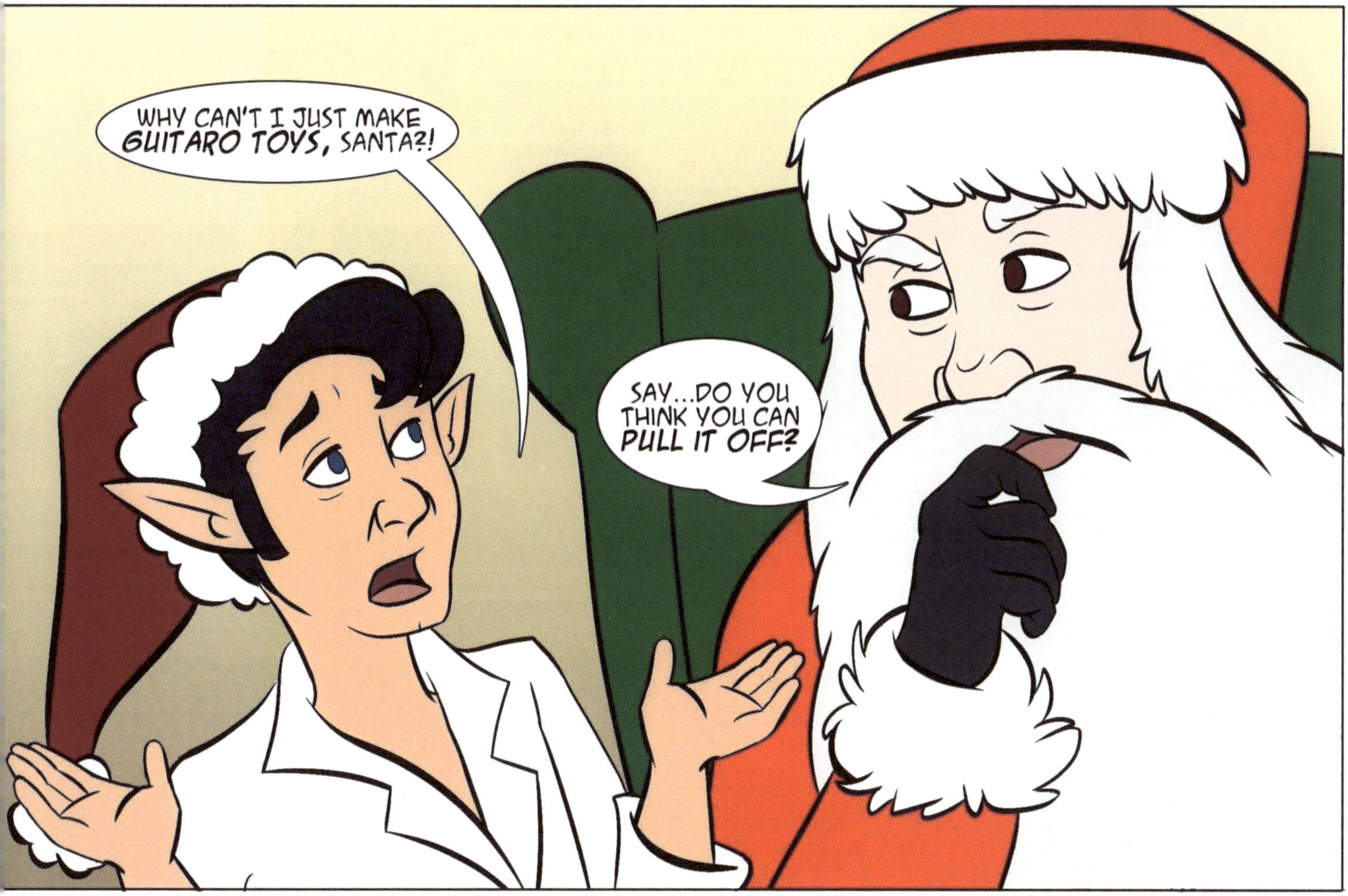
WHY CAN'T I JUST MAKE GUITARO TOYS, SANTA?!
SAY...DO YOU THINK YOU CAN PULL IT OFF?

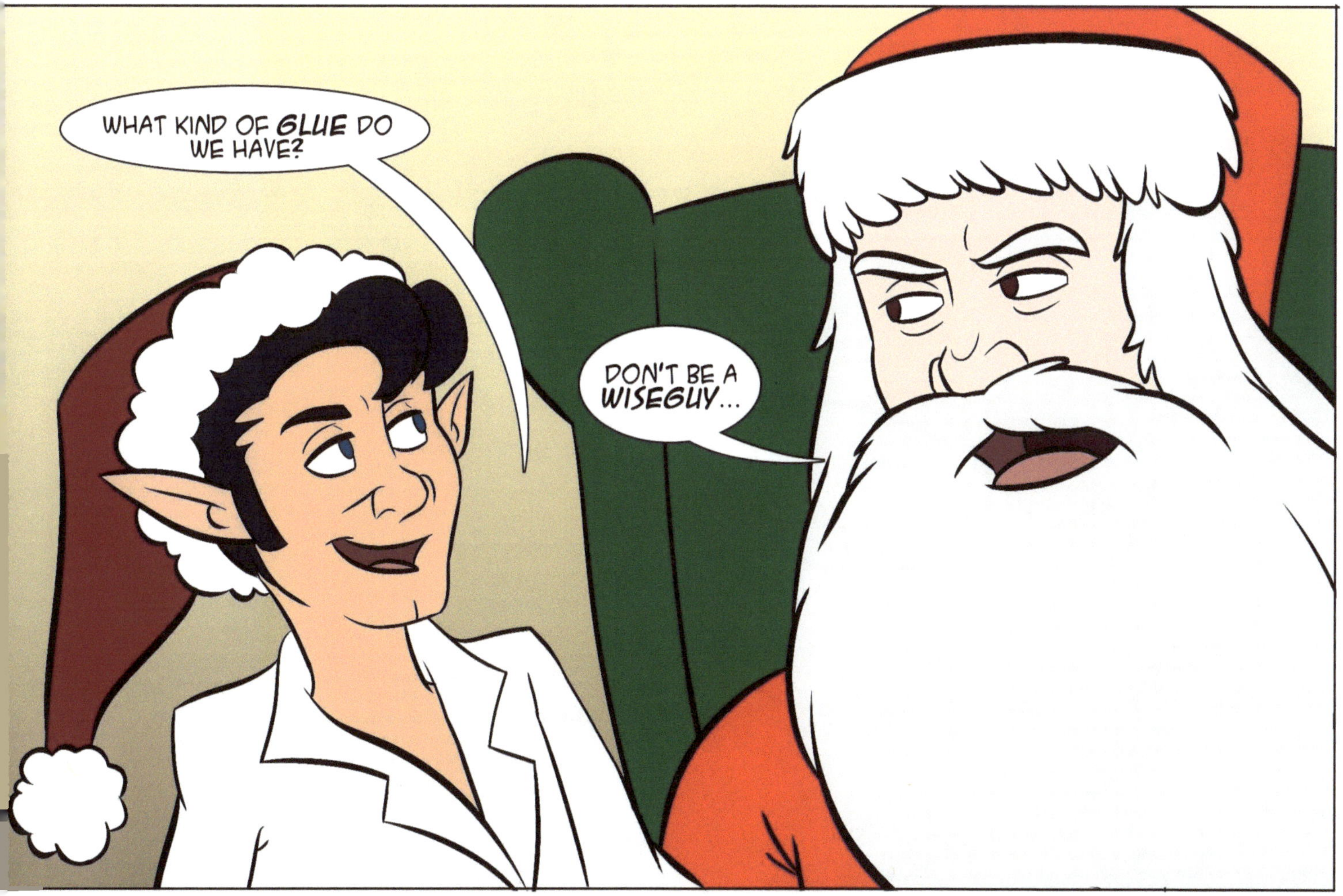
WHAT KIND OF GLUE DO WE HAVE?
DON'T BE A WISEGUY...

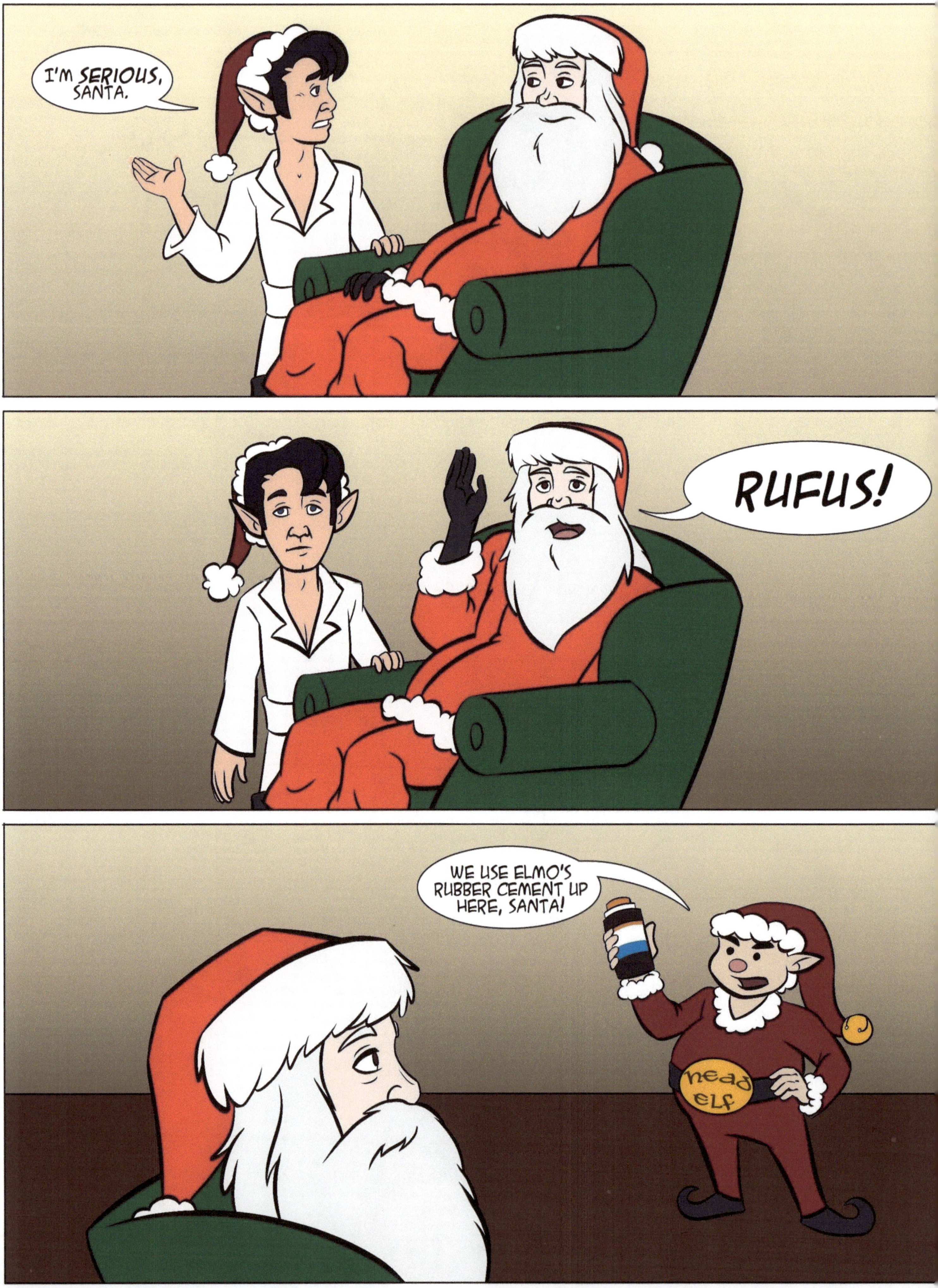
I'M SERIOUS, SANTA.
RUFUS!
WE USE ELMO'S RUBBER CEMENT UP HERE, SANTA!
head elf

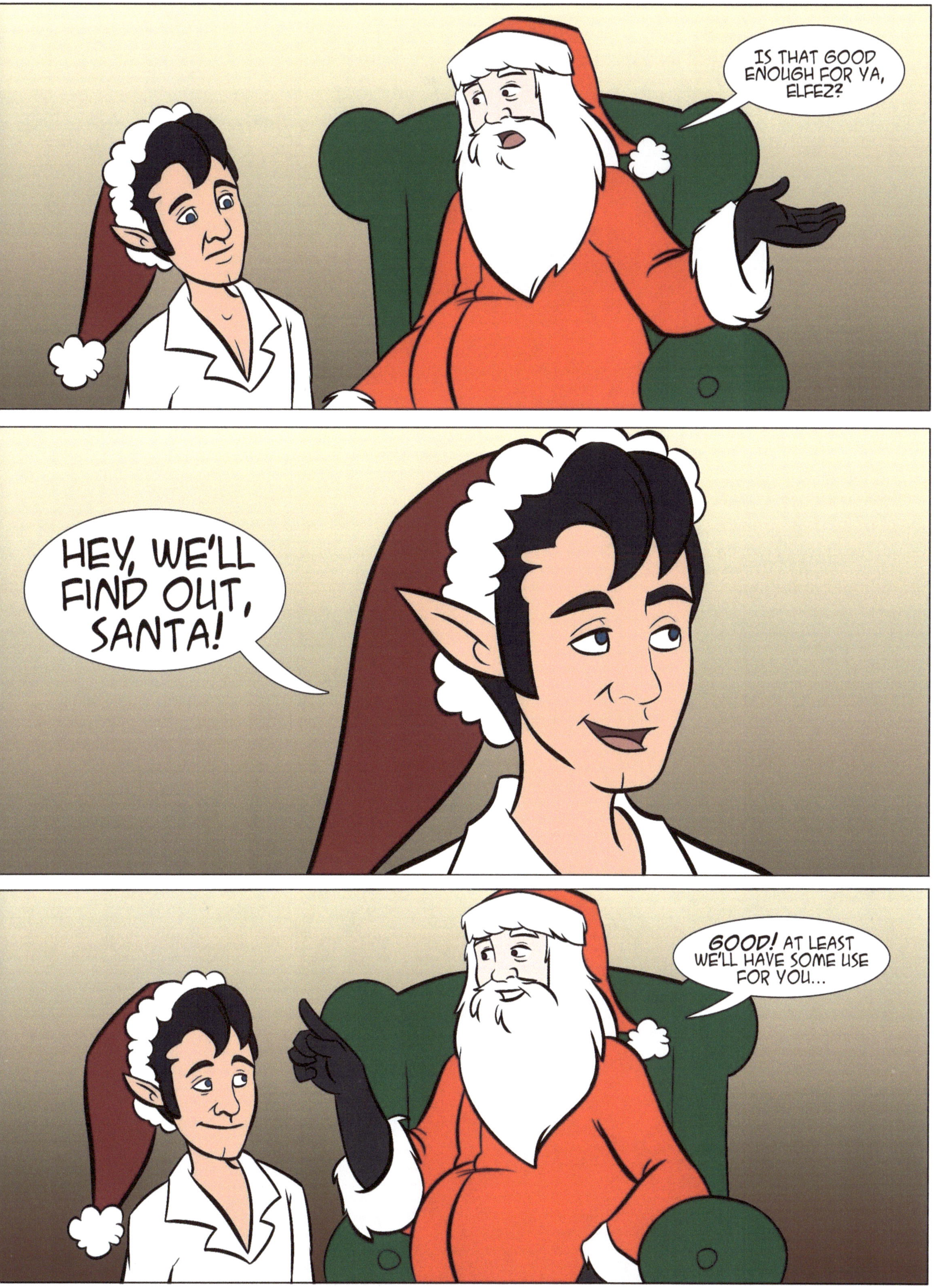
IS THAT GOOD ENOUGH FOR YA, ELFEZ?
HEY, WE'LL FIND OUT, SANTA!
GOOD! AT LEAST WE'LL HAVE SOME USE FOR YOU...

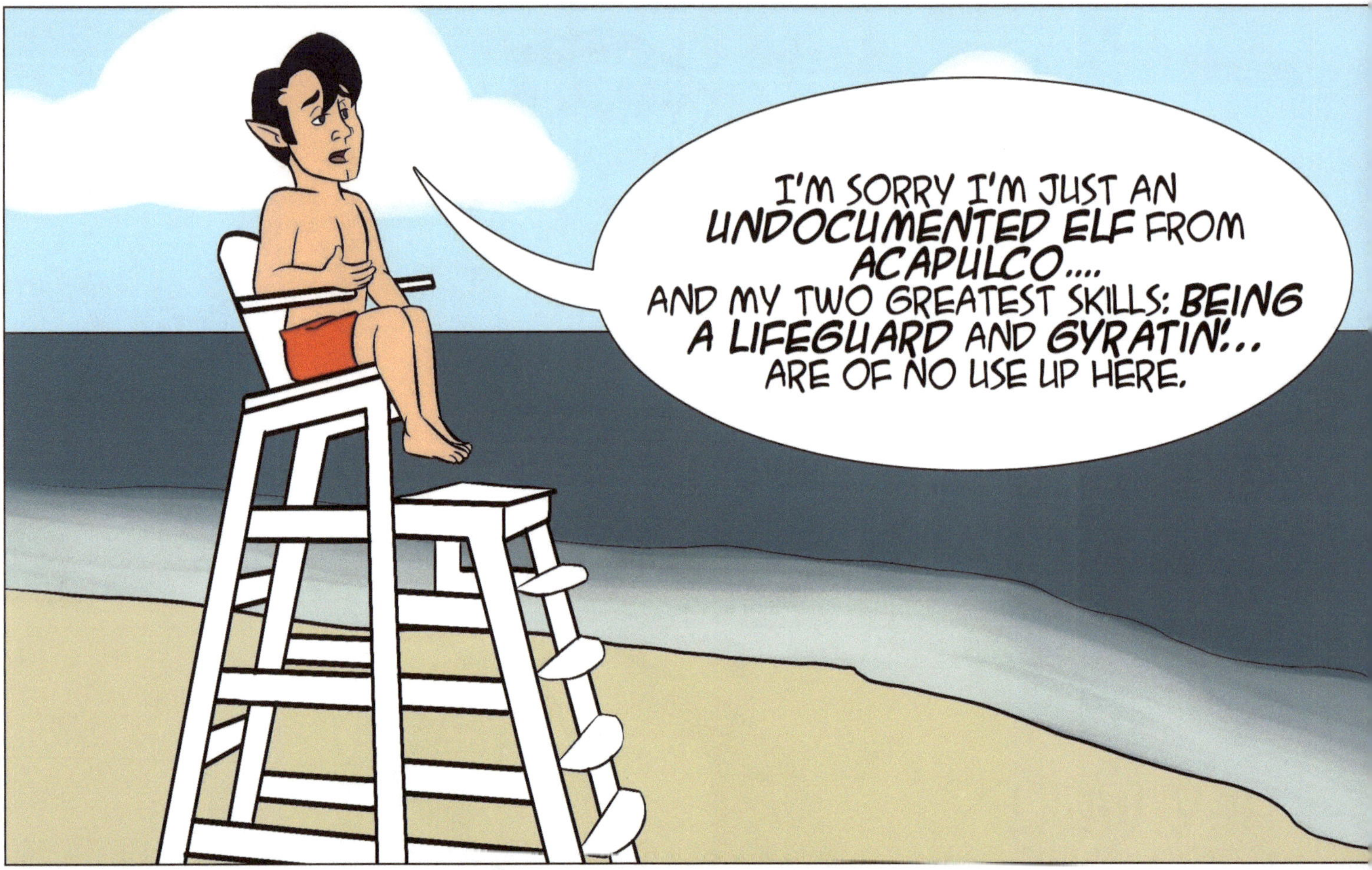
I'M SORRY I'M JUST AN **UNDOCUMENTED ELF** FROM **ACAPULCO**.... AND MY TWO GREATEST SKILLS: **BEING A LIFEGUARD** AND **GYRATIN'**... ARE OF NO USE UP HERE.

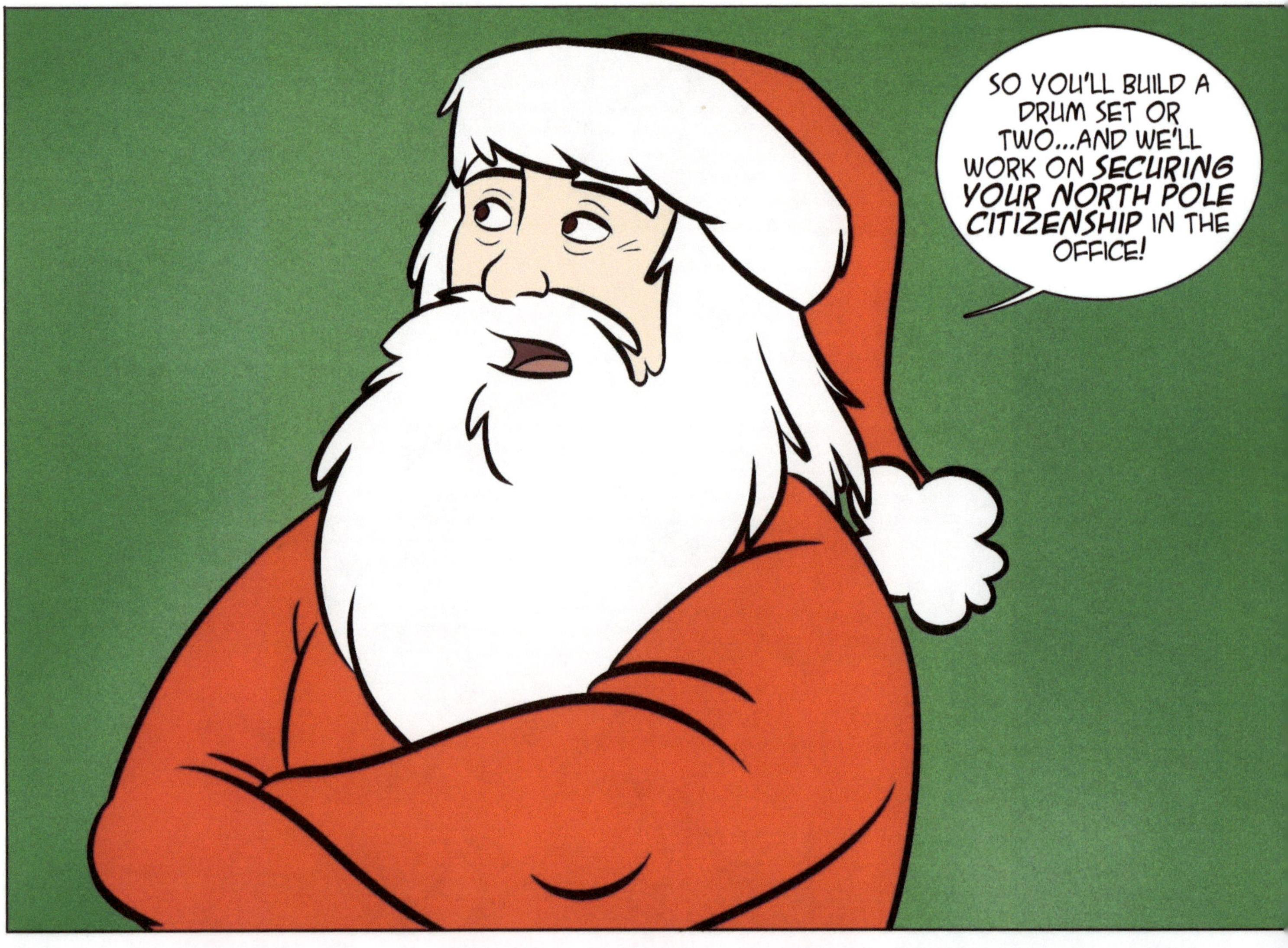
SO YOU'LL BUILD A DRUM SET OR TWO...AND WE'LL WORK ON **SECURING YOUR NORTH POLE CITIZENSHIP** IN THE OFFICE!

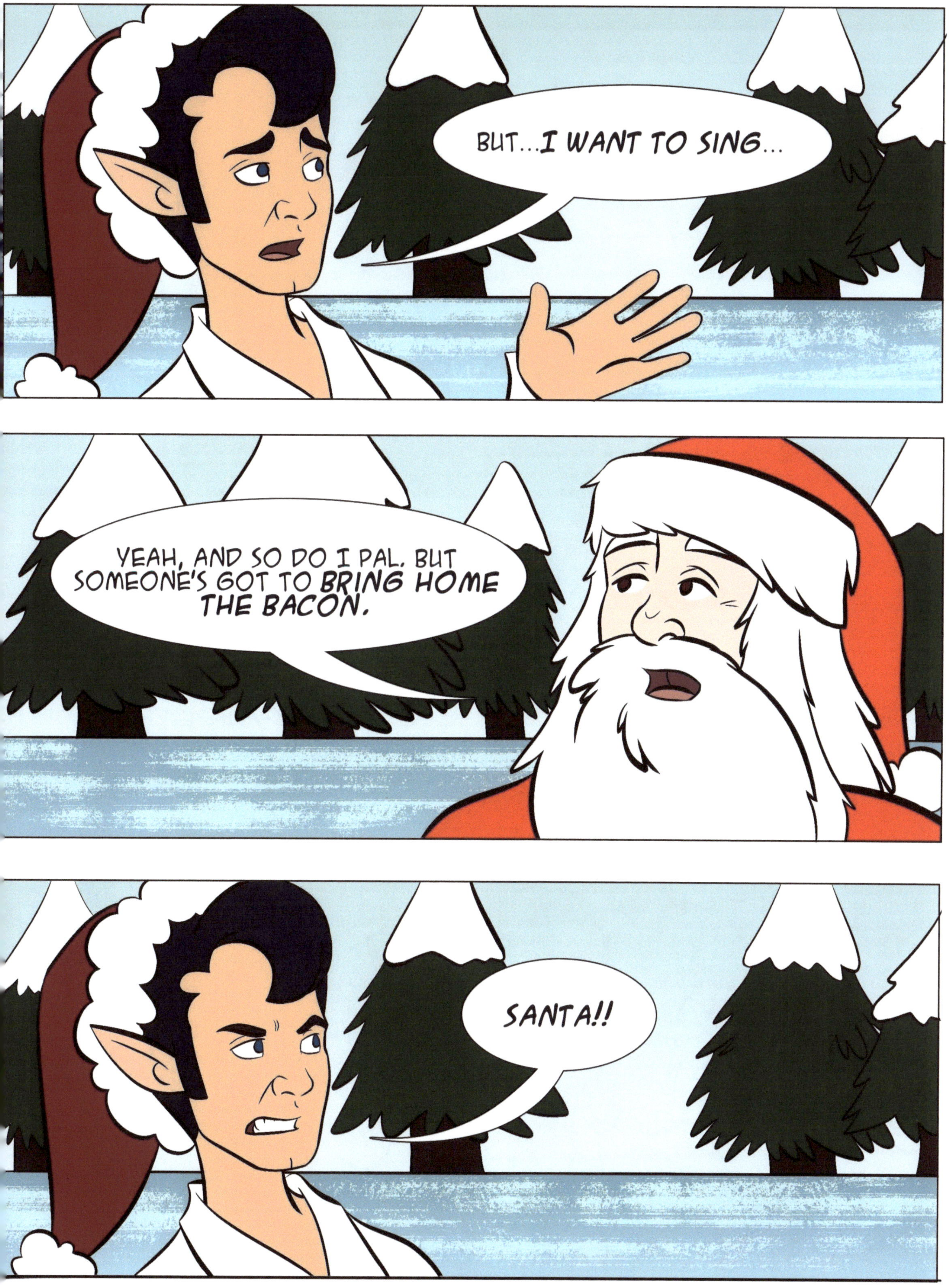
BUT...I WANT TO SING...
YEAH, AND SO DO I PAL. BUT SOMEONE'S GOT TO BRING HOME THE BACON.
SANTA!!

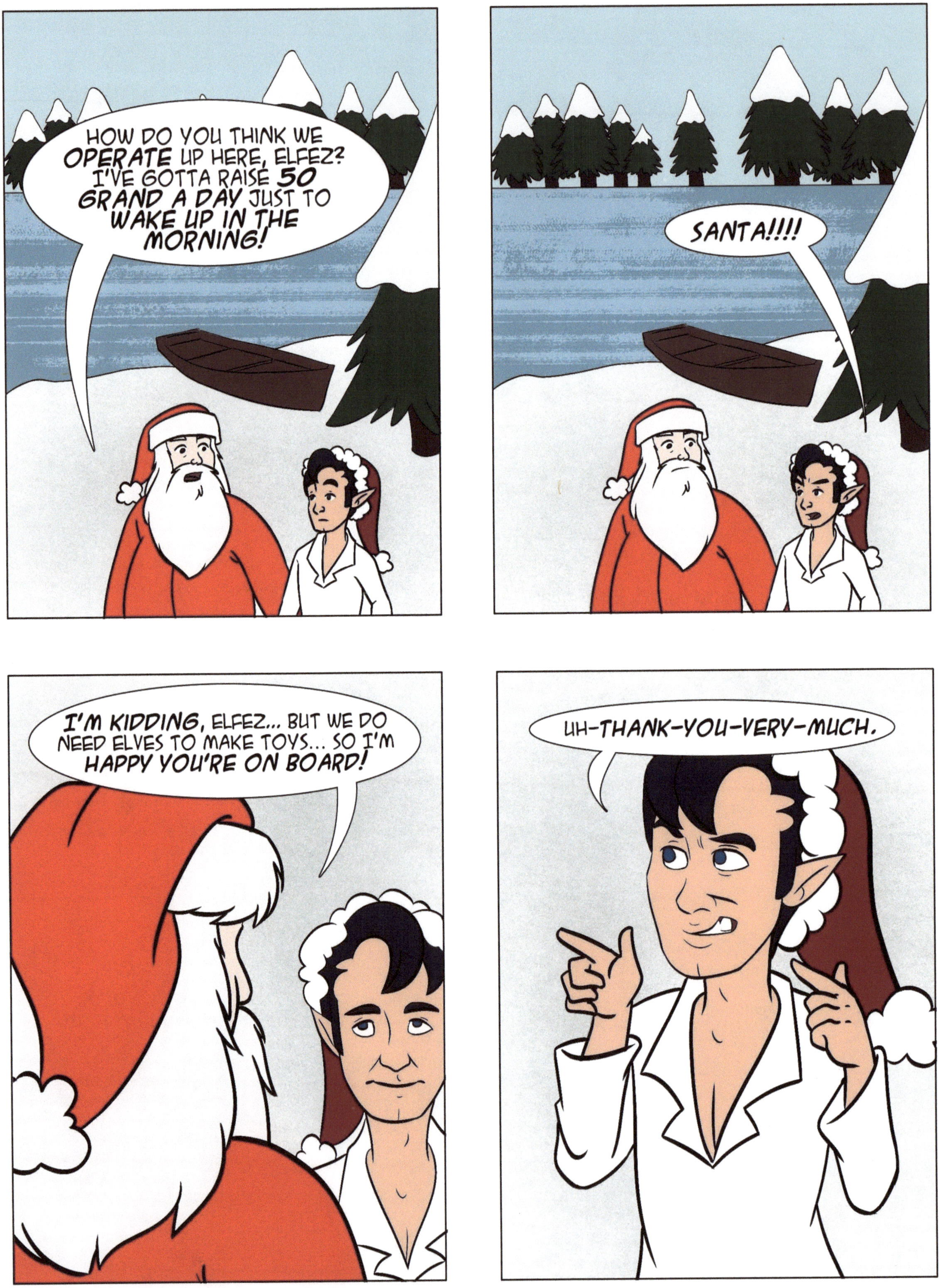
HOW DO YOU THINK WE OPERATE UP HERE, ELFEZ? I'VE GOTTA RAISE 50 GRAND A DAY JUST TO WAKE UP IN THE MORNING!
SANTA!!!!
I'M KIDDING, ELFEZ... BUT WE DO NEED ELVES TO MAKE TOYS... SO I'M HAPPY YOU'RE ON BOARD!
UH-THANK-YOU-VERY-MUCH.

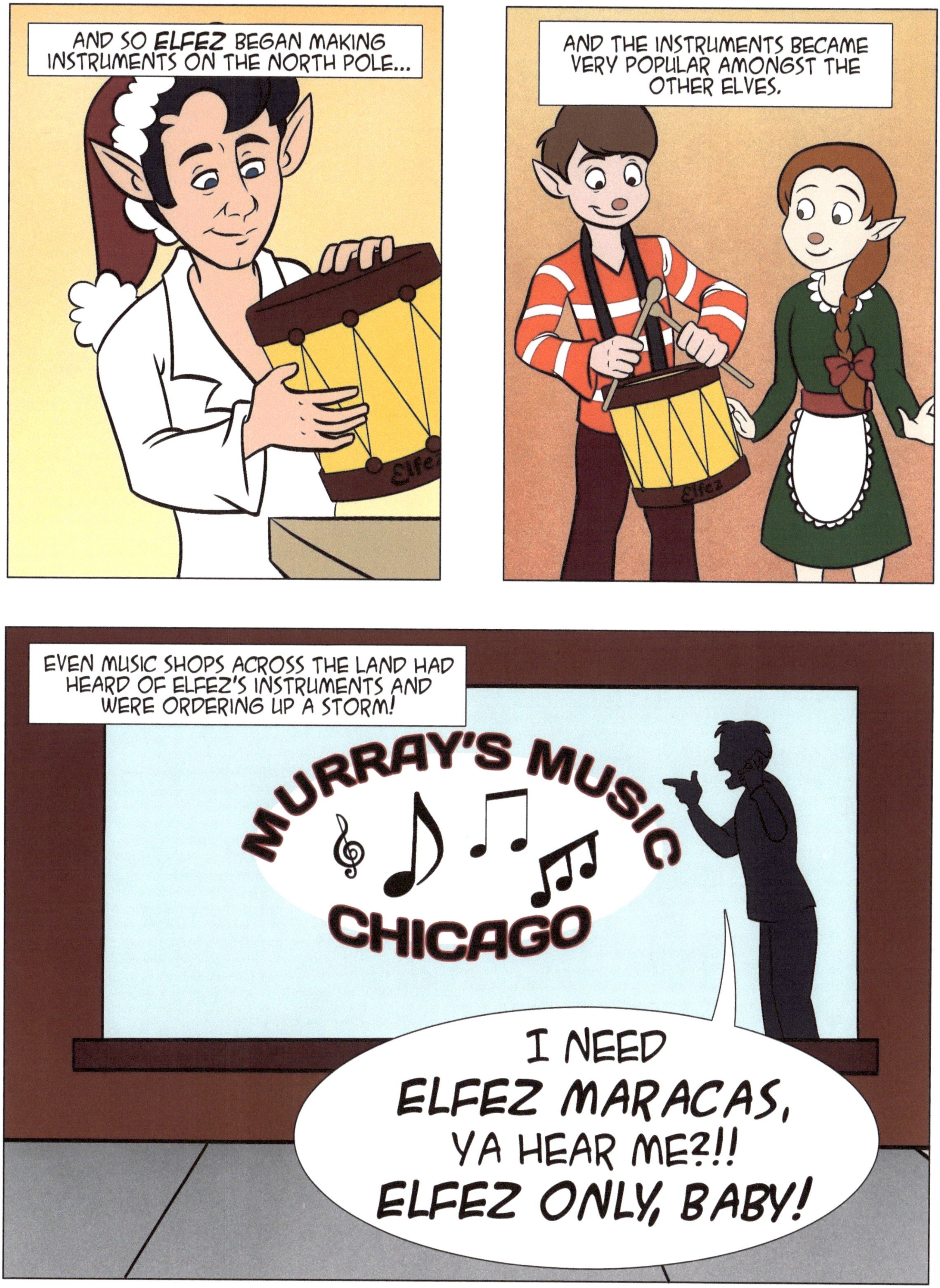
AND SO ELFEZ BEGAN MAKING INSTRUMENTS ON THE NORTH POLE...
Elfez
AND THE INSTRUMENTS BECAME VERY POPULAR AMONGST THE OTHER ELVES.
Elfez
EVEN MUSIC SHOPS ACROSS THE LAND HAD HEARD OF ELFEZ'S INSTRUMENTS AND WERE ORDERING UP A STORM!
MURRAY'S MUSIC
CHICAGO
I NEED ELFEZ MARACAS, YA HEAR ME?!! ELFEZ ONLY, BABY!

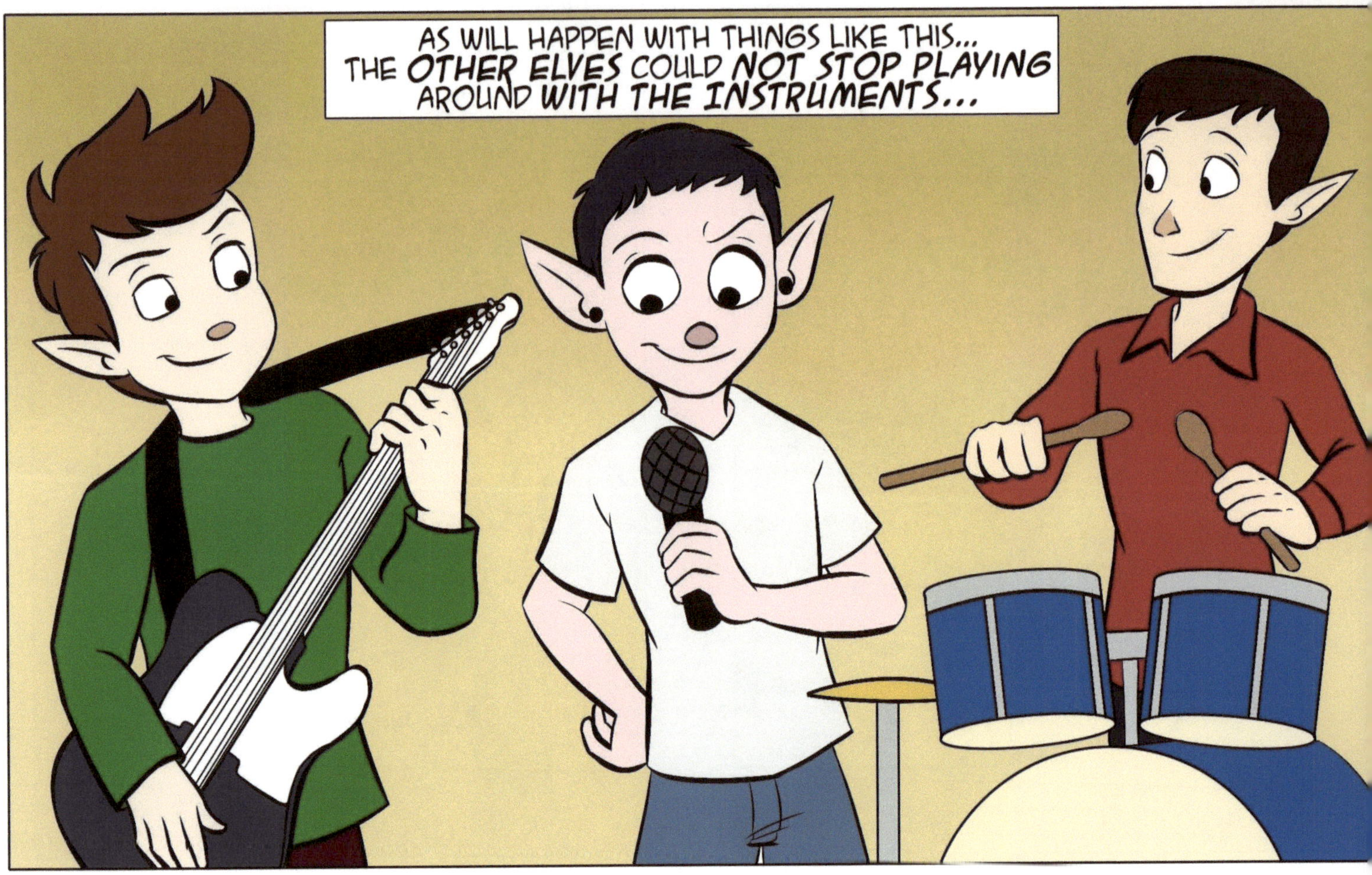
AS WILL HAPPEN WITH THINGS LIKE THIS... THE OTHER ELVES COULD NOT STOP PLAYING AROUND WITH THE INSTRUMENTS...

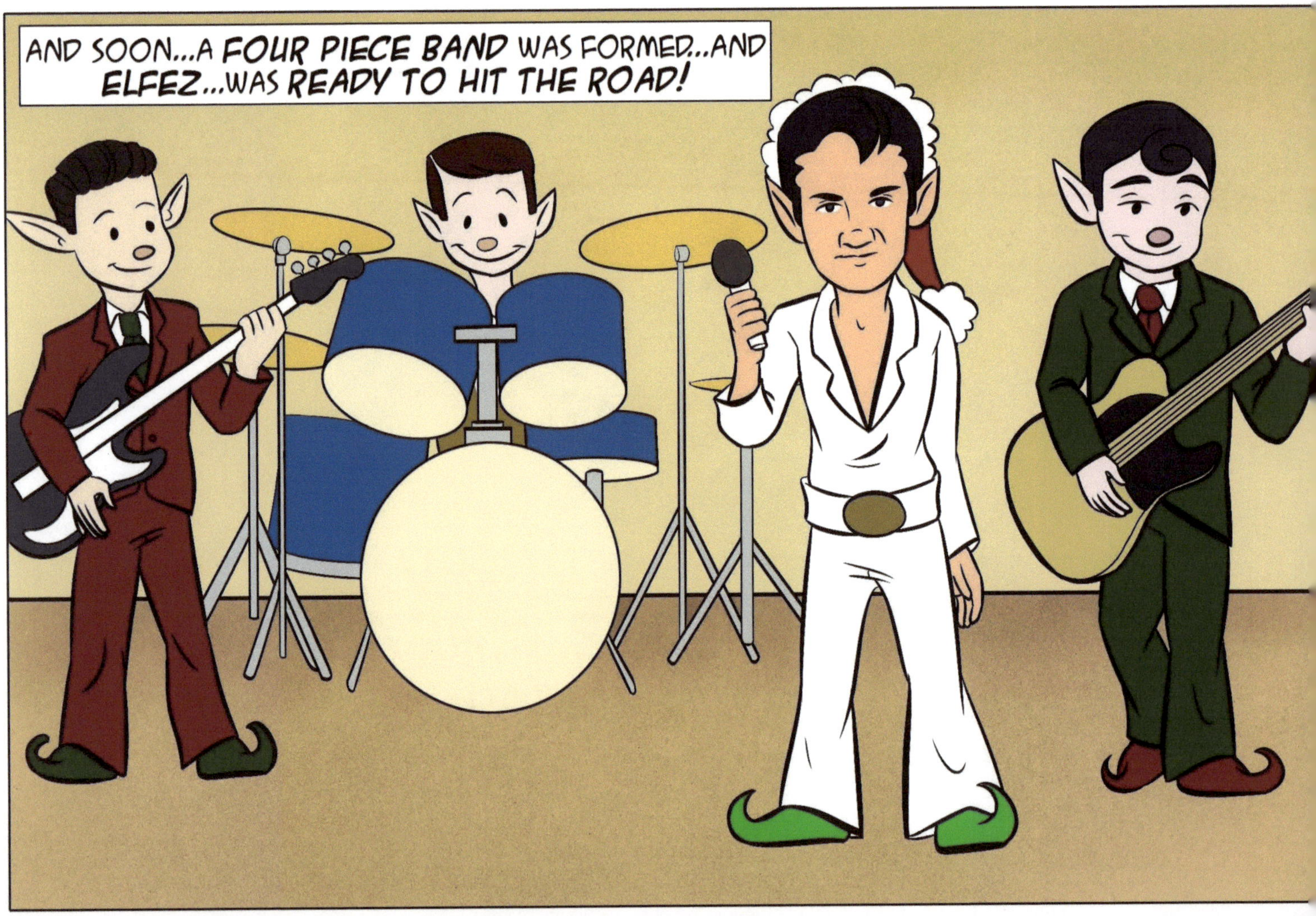
AND SOON...A FOUR PIECE BAND WAS FORMED...AND ELFEZ...WAS READY TO HIT THE ROAD!

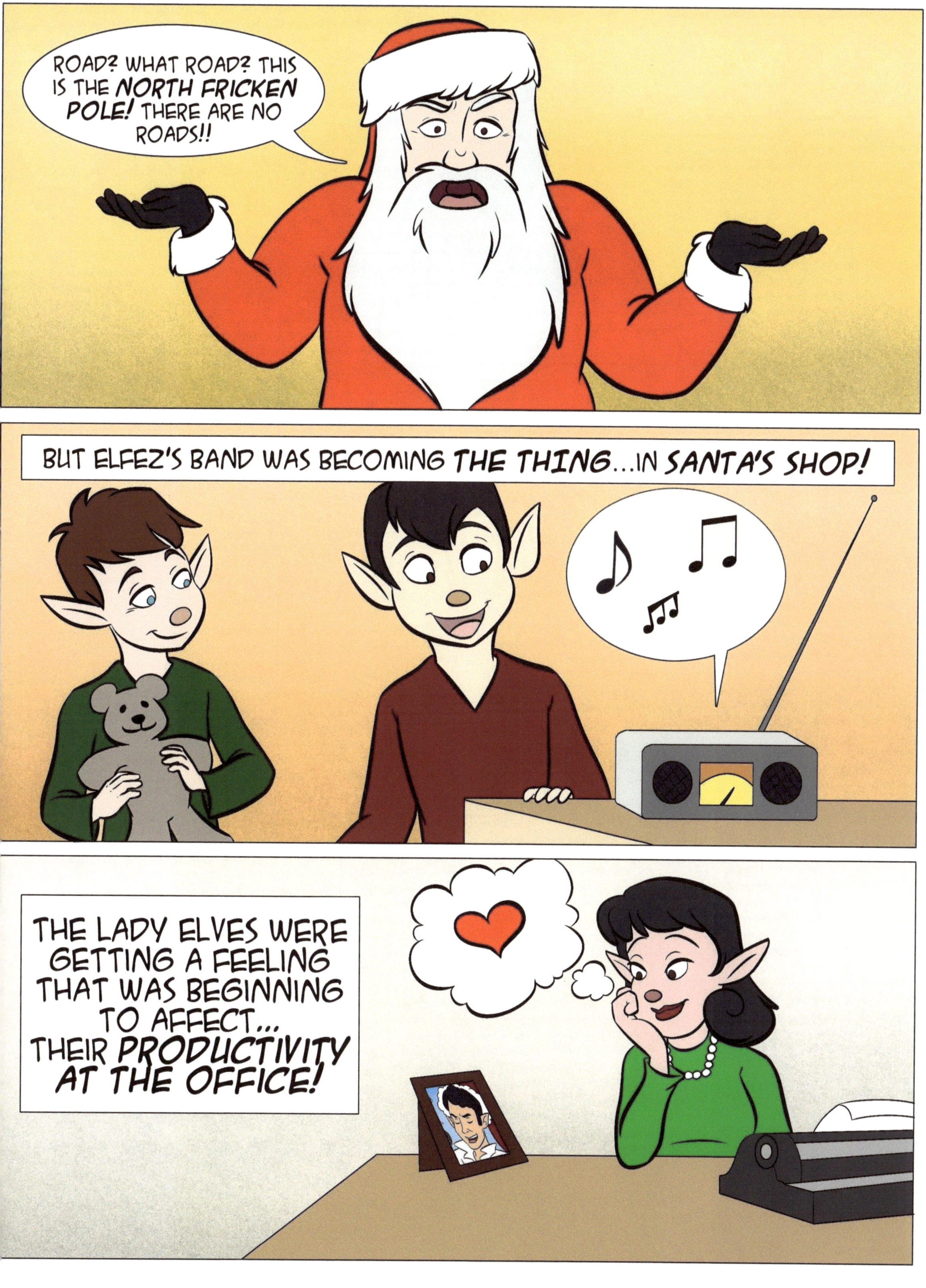
ROAD? WHAT ROAD? THIS IS THE NORTH FRICKEN POLE! THERE ARE NO ROADS!!
BUT ELFEZ'S BAND WAS BECOMING THE THING...IN SANTA'S SHOP!
THE LADY ELVES WERE GETTING A FEELING THAT WAS BEGINNING TO AFFECT... THEIR PRODUCTIVITY AT THE OFFICE!

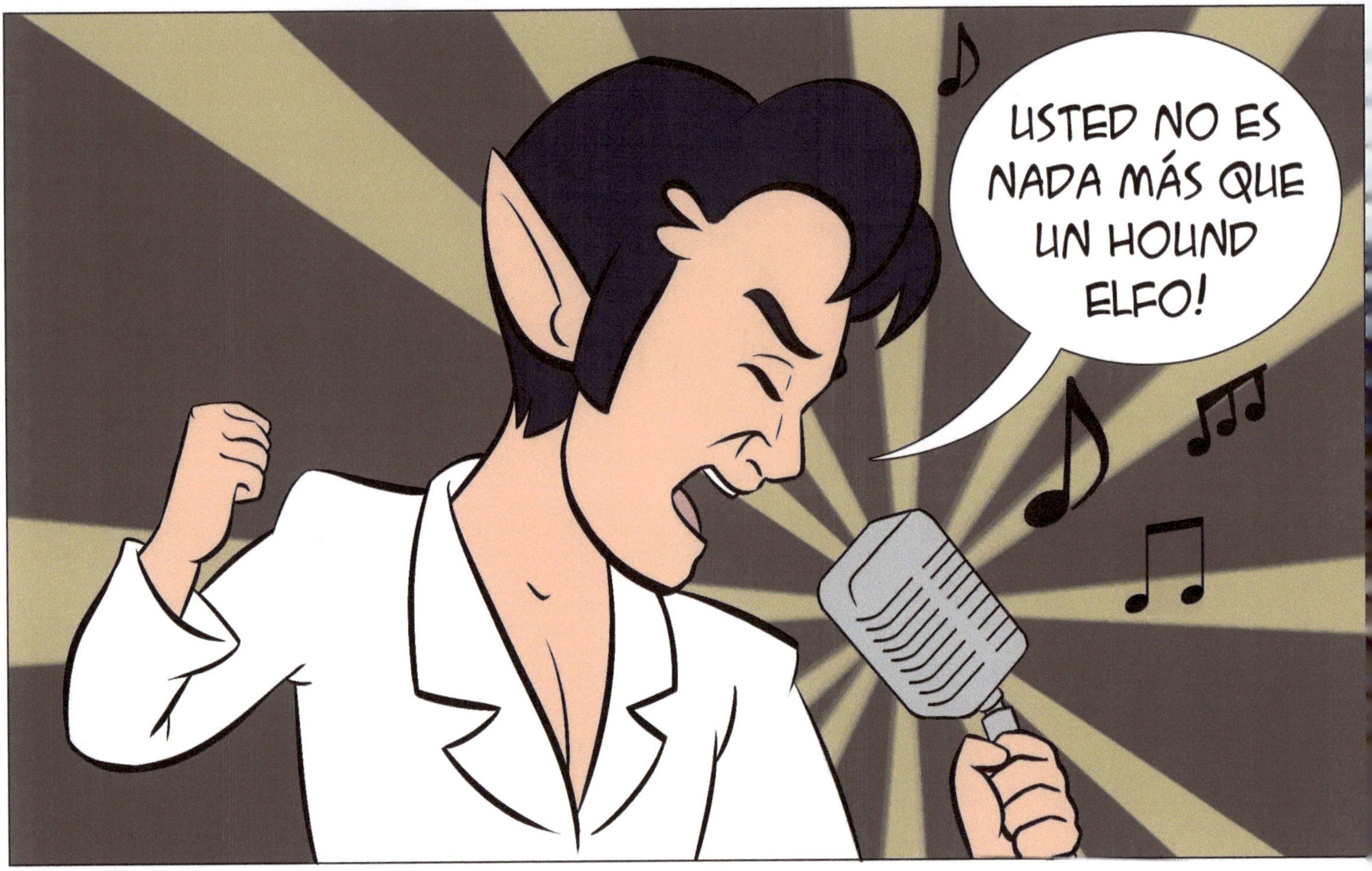
USTED NO ES NADA MÁS QUE UN HOUND ELFO!

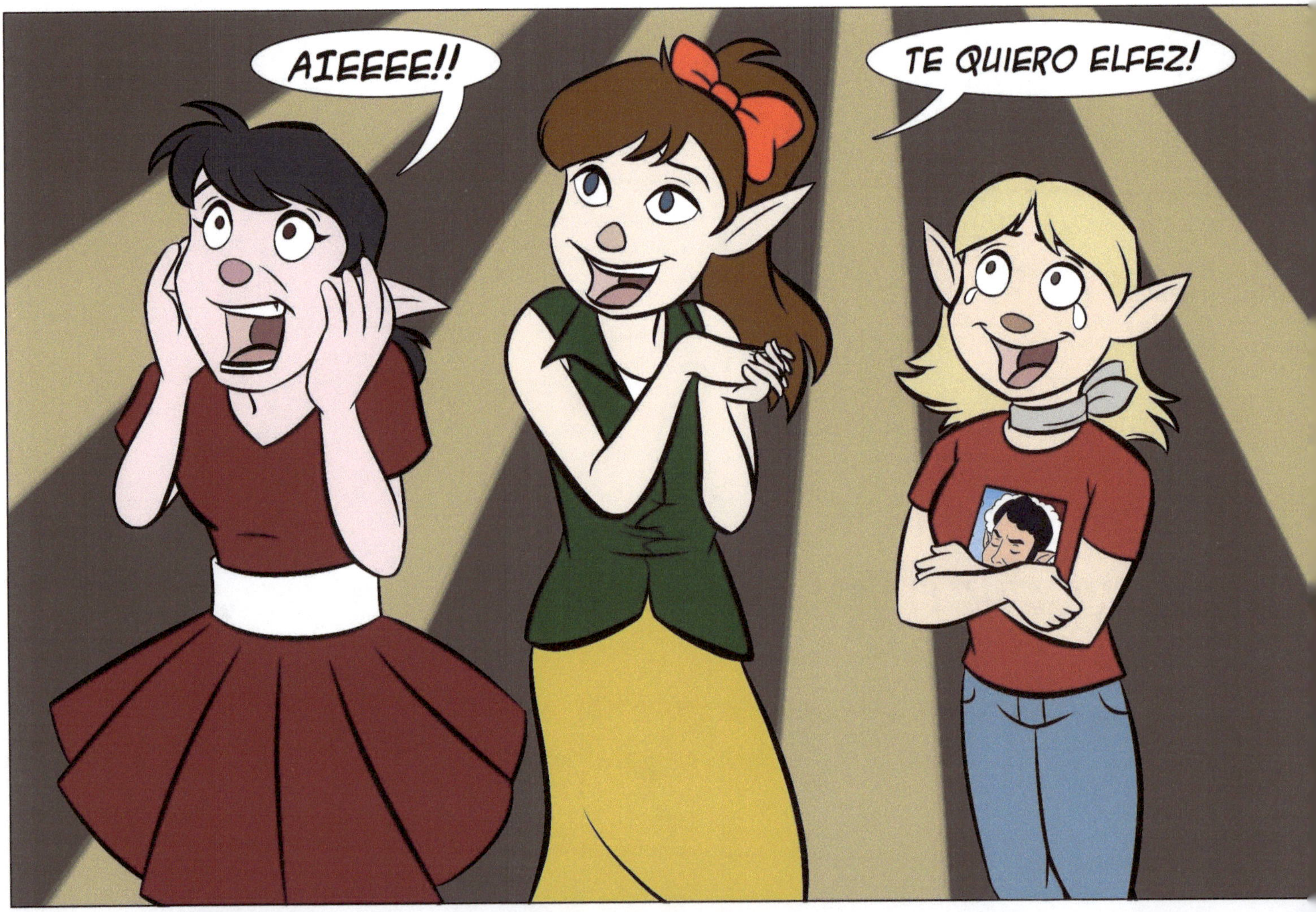
AIEEEEE!!
TE QUIERO ELFEZ!

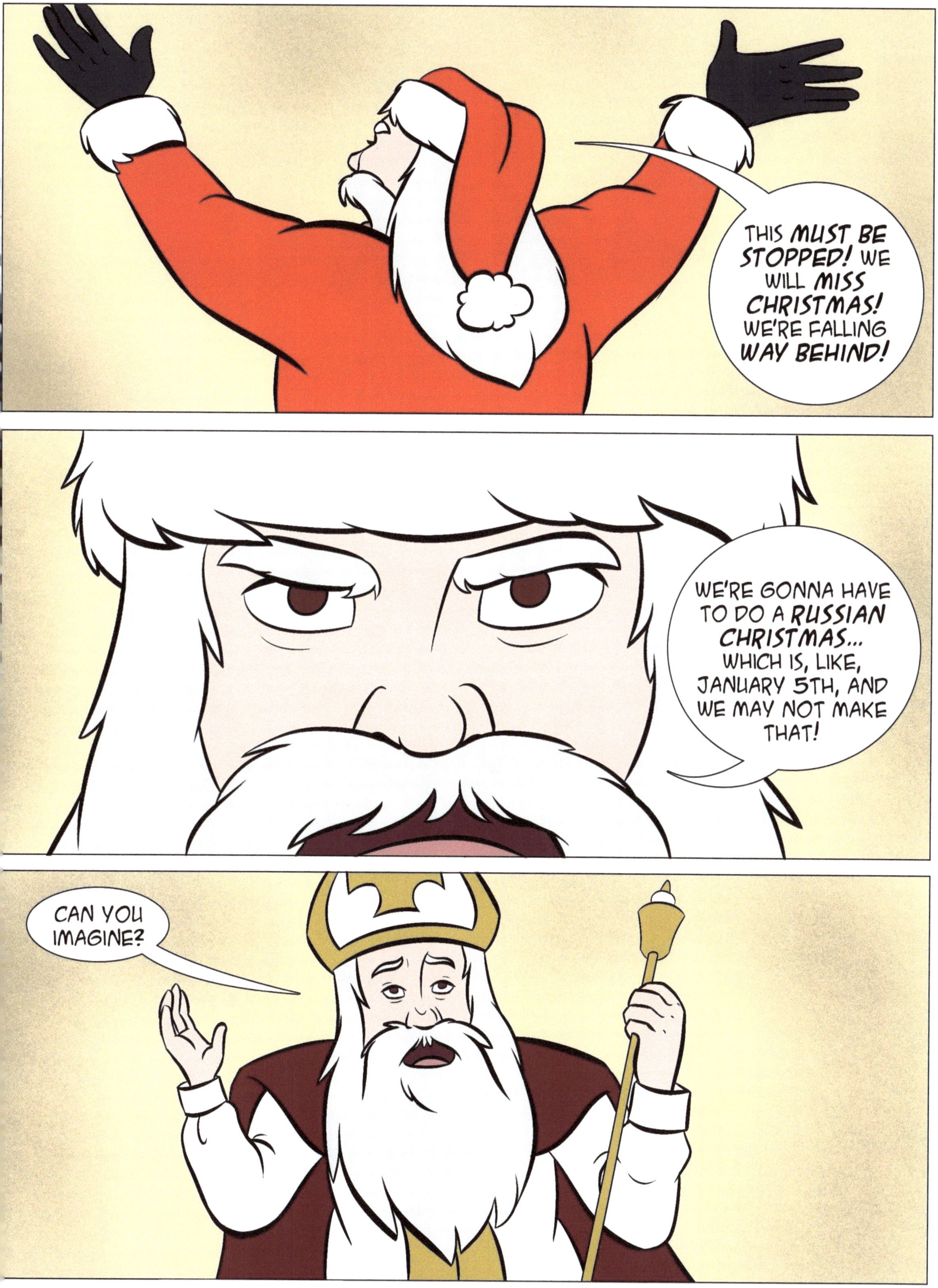
THIS MUST BE STOPPED! WE WILL MISS CHRISTMAS! WE'RE FALLING WAY BEHIND!
WE'RE GONNA HAVE TO DO A RUSSIAN CHRISTMAS... WHICH IS, LIKE, JANUARY 5TH, AND WE MAY NOT MAKE THAT!
CAN YOU IMAGINE?

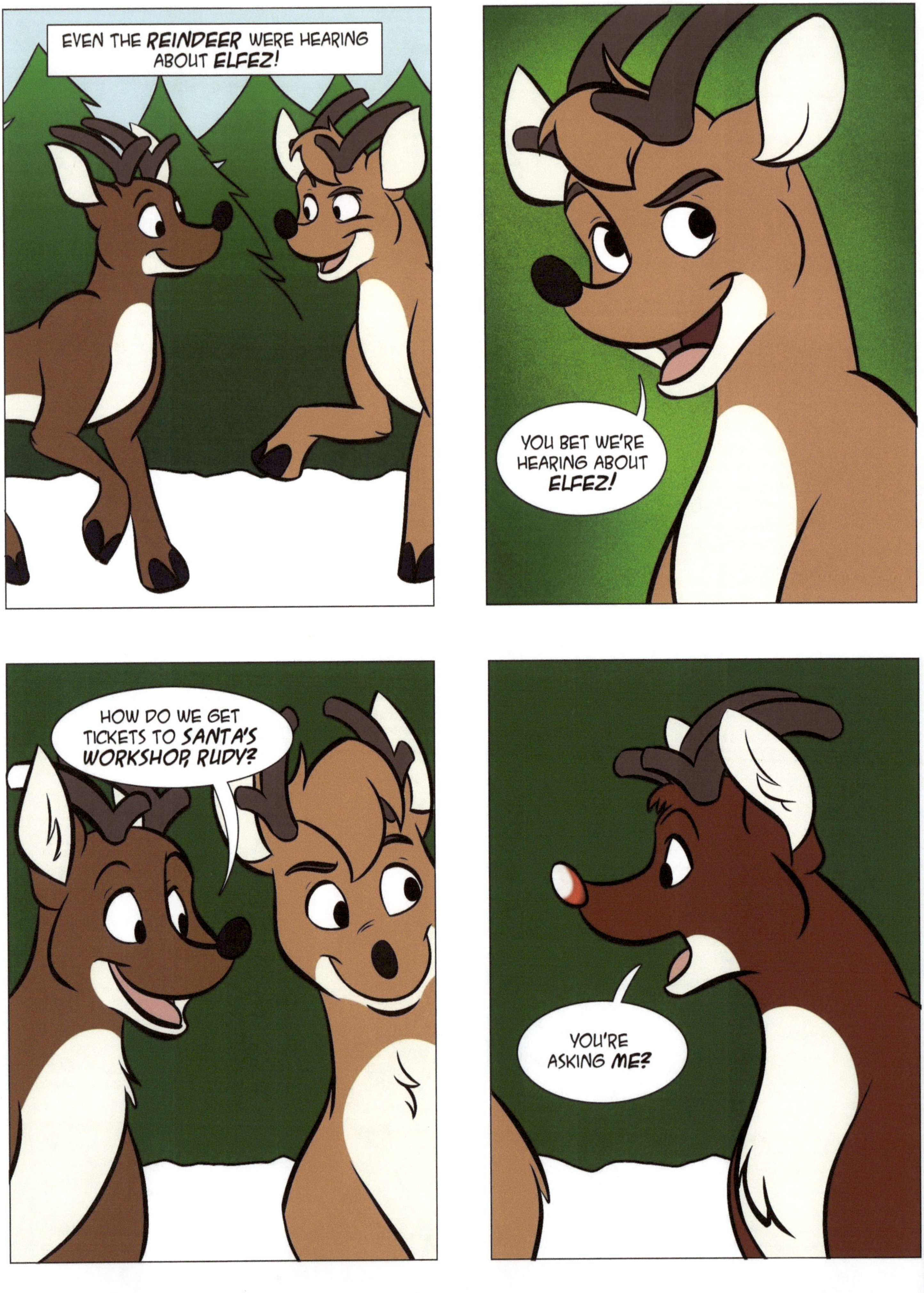
EVEN THE REINDEER WERE HEARING ABOUT ELFEZ!
YOU BET WE'RE HEARING ABOUT ELFEZ!
HOW DO WE GET TICKETS TO SANTA'S WORKSHOP, RUDY?
YOU'RE ASKING ME?

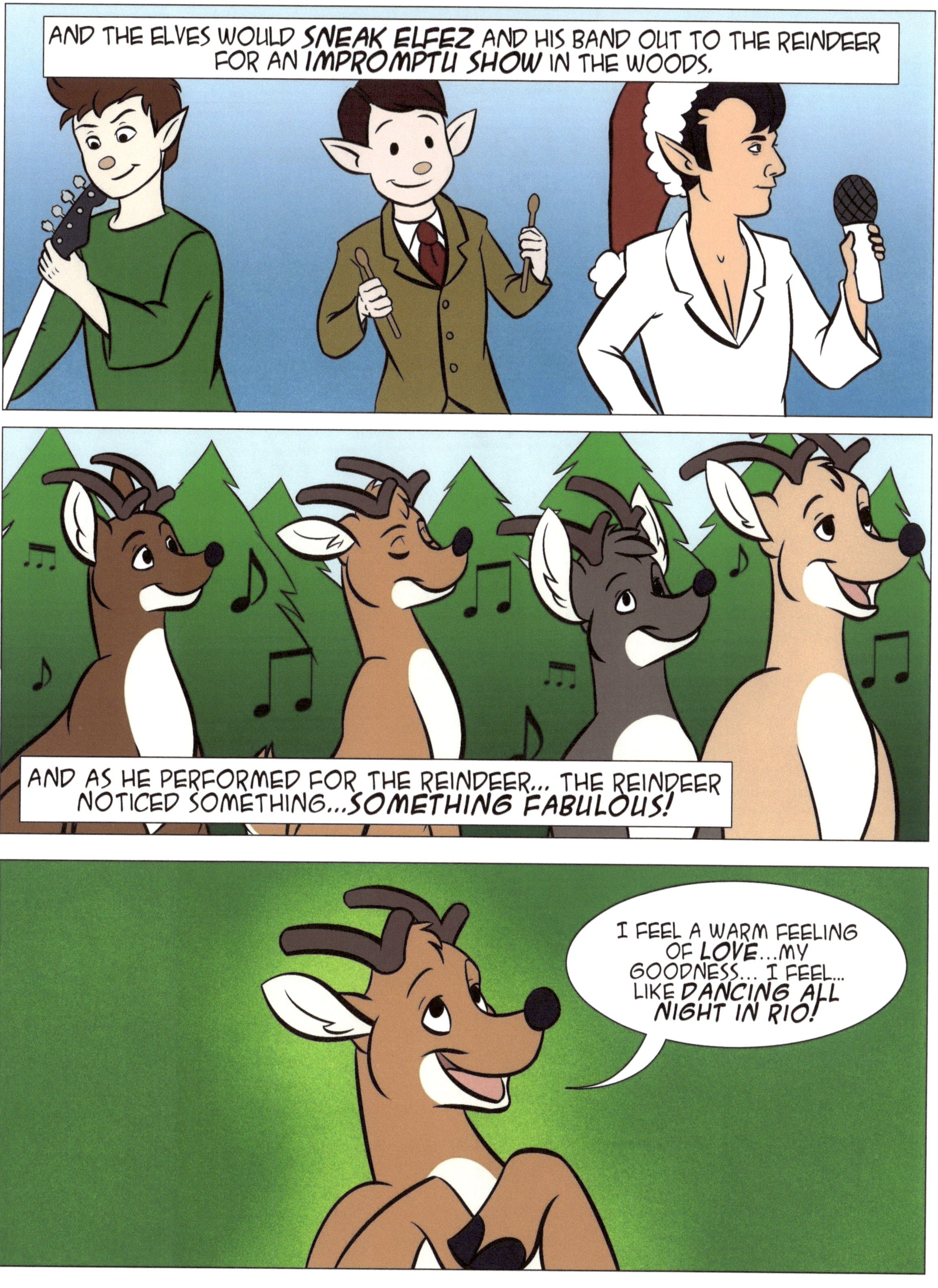
AND THE ELVES WOULD SNEAK ELFEZ AND HIS BAND OUT TO THE REINDEER FOR AN IMPROMPTU SHOW IN THE WOODS.
AND AS HE PERFORMED FOR THE REINDEER... THE REINDEER NOTICED SOMETHING...SOMETHING FABULOUS!
I FEEL A WARM FEELING OF LOVE...MY GOODNESS... I FEEL... LIKE DANCING ALL NIGHT IN RIO!

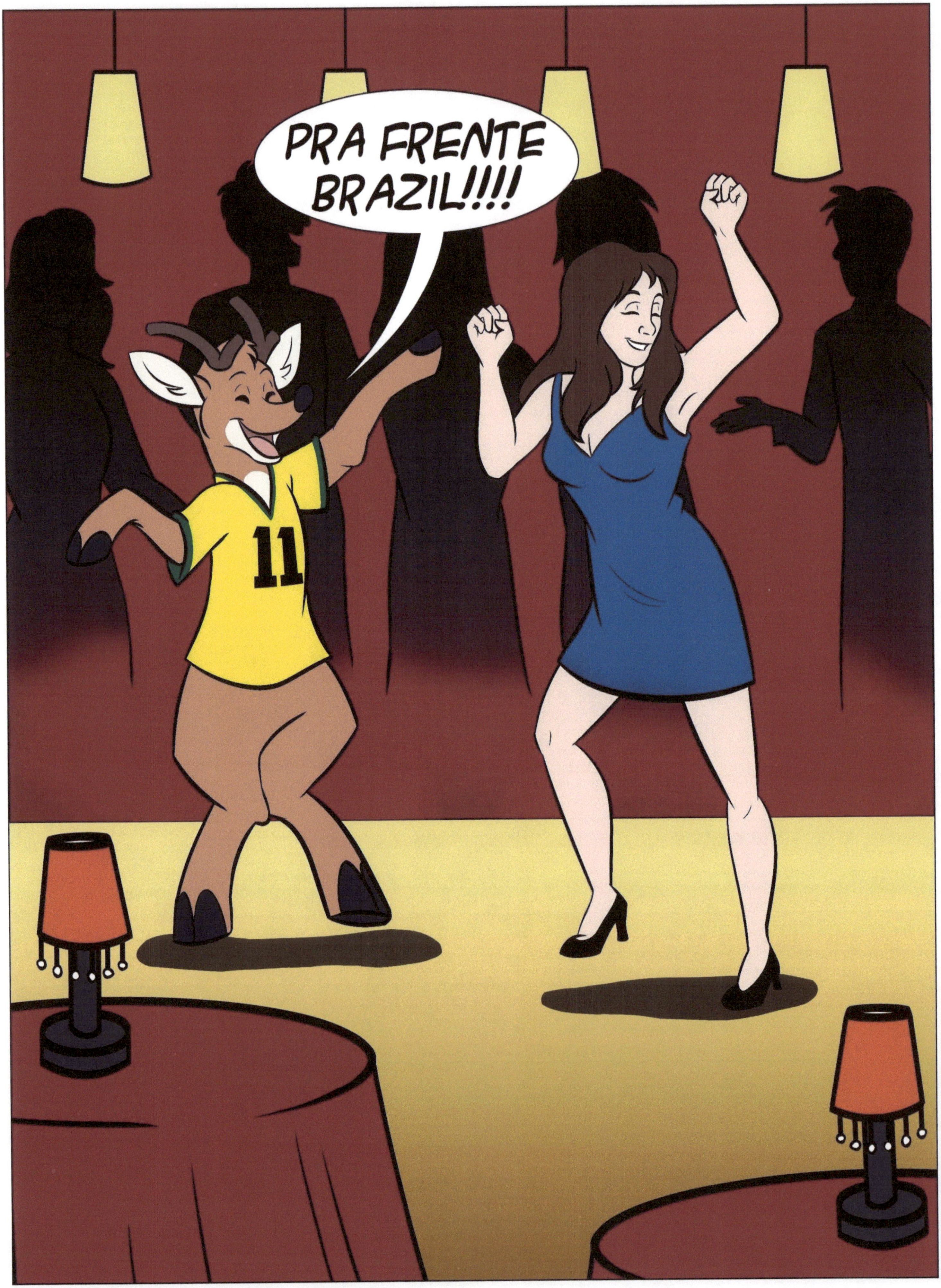
PRA FRENTE BRAZIL!!!!
11

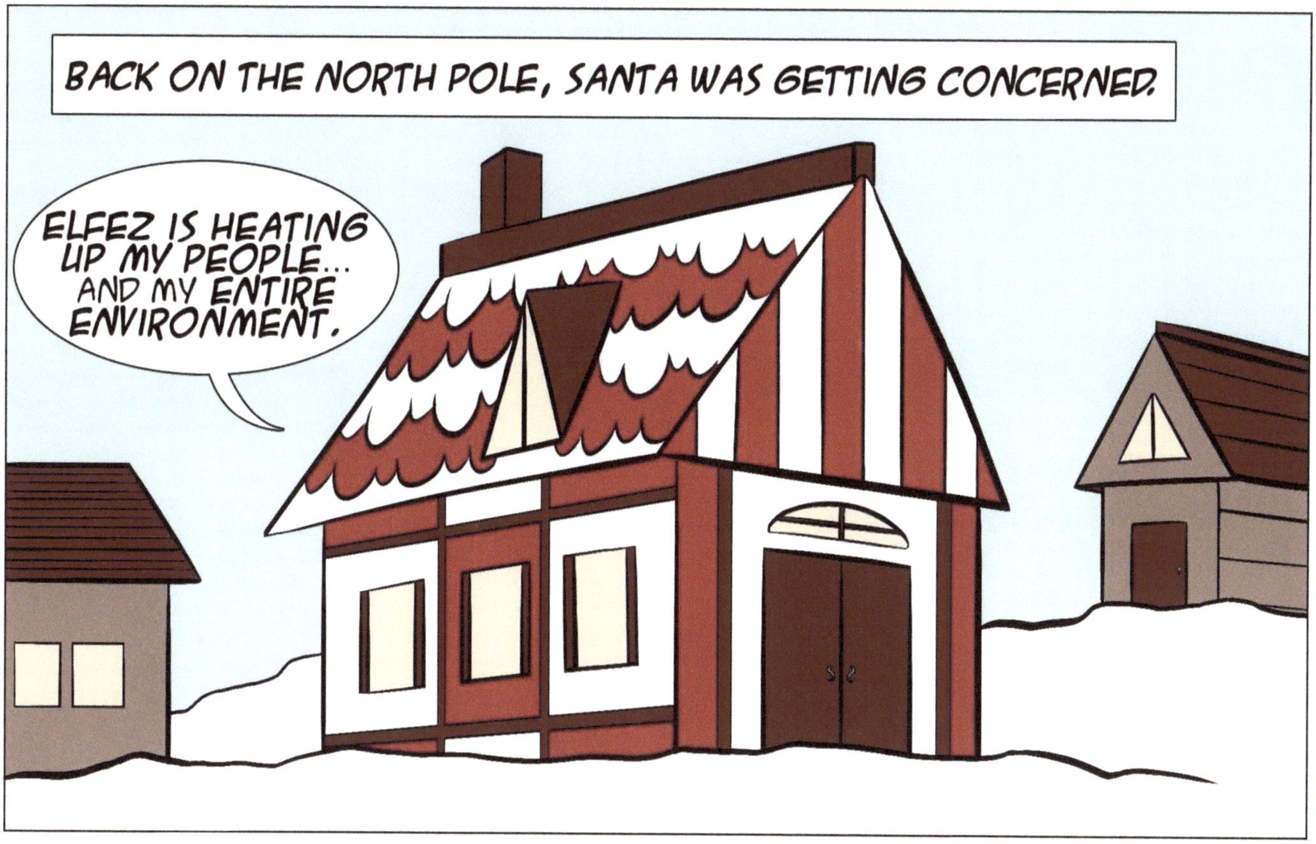
BACK ON THE NORTH POLE, SANTA WAS GETTING CONCERNED.
ELFEZ IS HEATING UP MY PEOPLE... AND MY ENTIRE ENVIRONMENT.

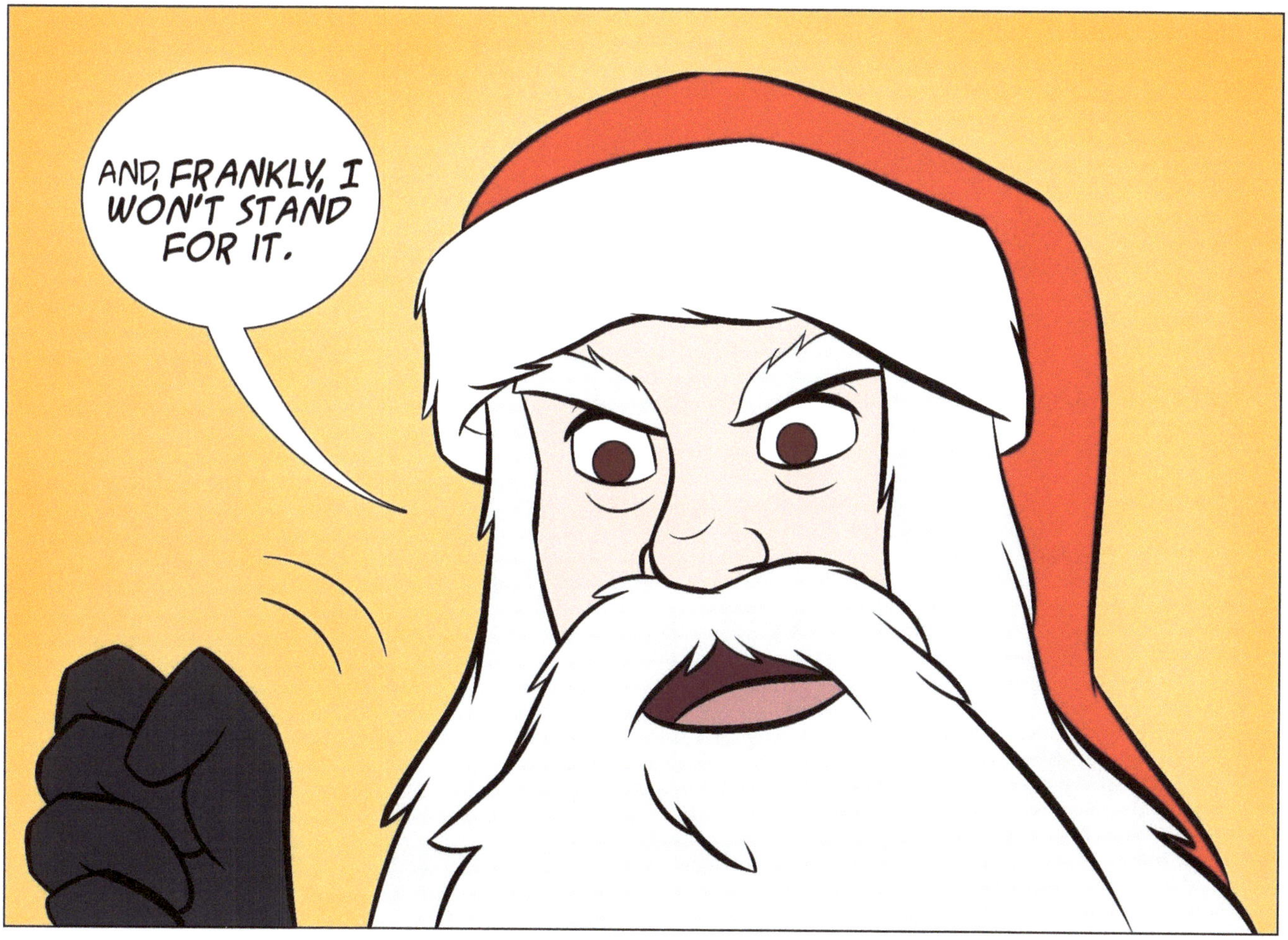
AND, FRANKLY, I WON'T STAND FOR IT.

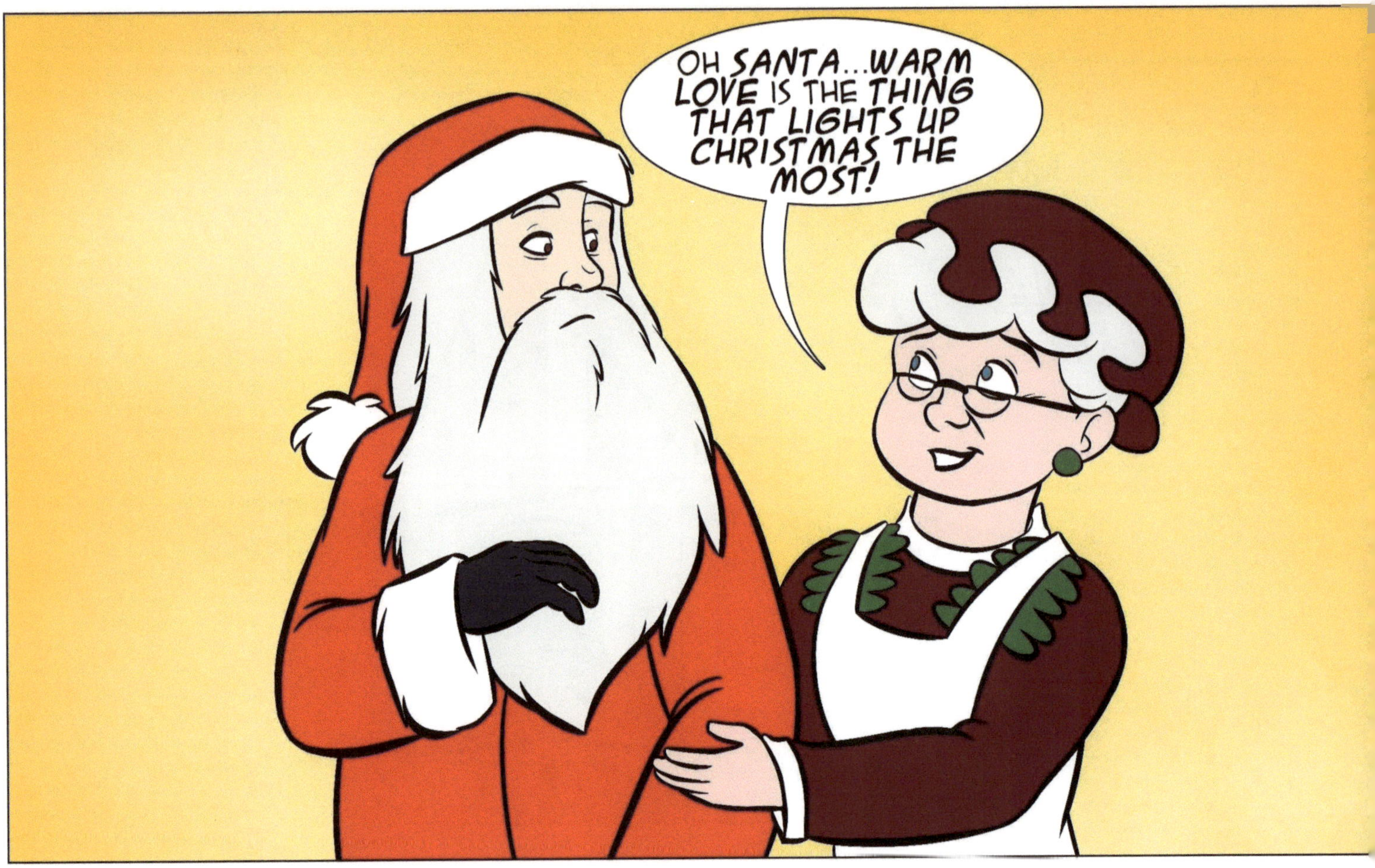
OH SANTA...WARM LOVE IS THE THING THAT LIGHTS UP CHRISTMAS THE MOST!

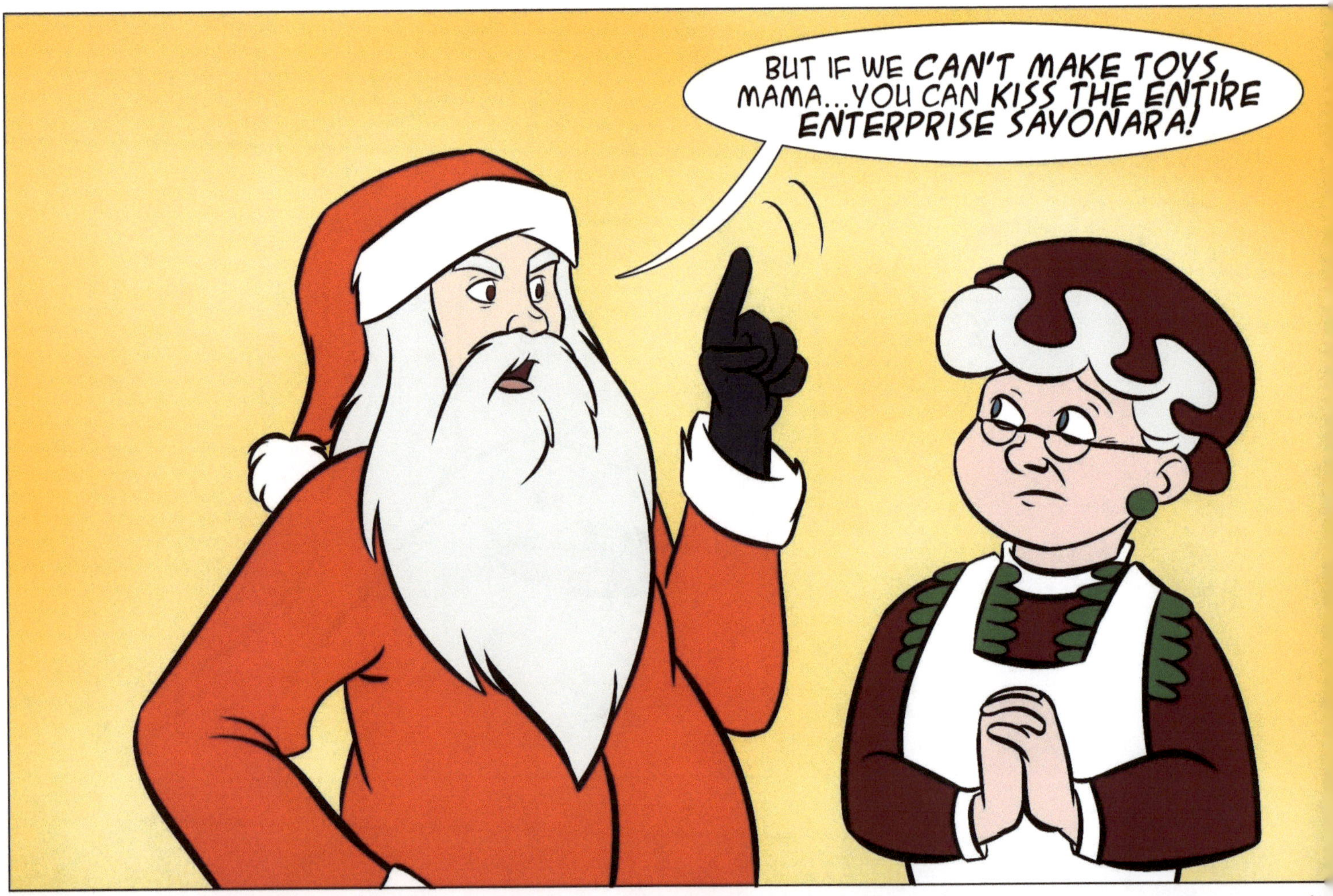
BUT IF WE CAN'T MAKE TOYS, MAMA...YOU CAN KISS THE ENTIRE ENTERPRISE SAYONARA!

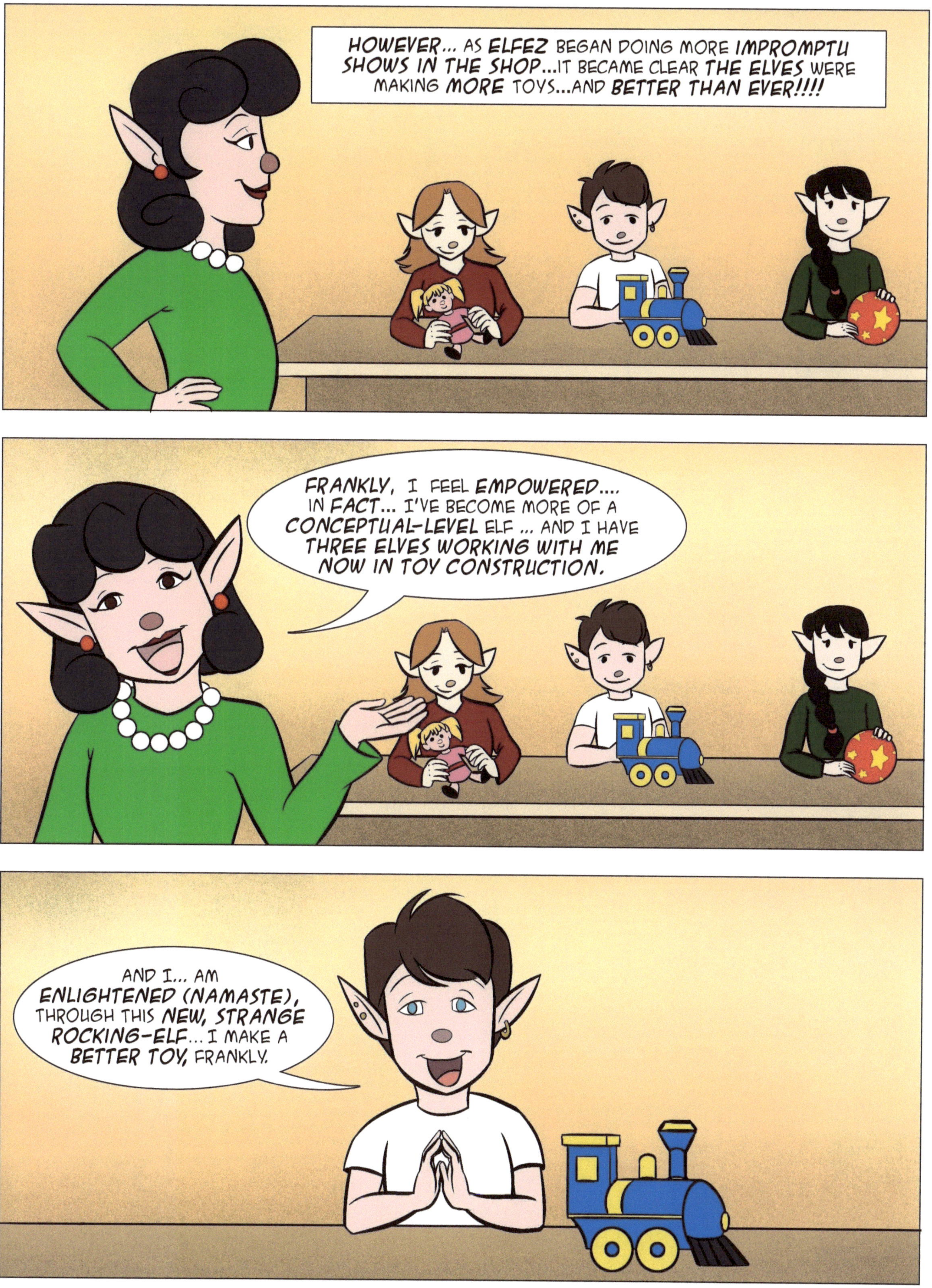
HOWEVER... AS ELFEZ BEGAN DOING MORE IMPROMPTU SHOWS IN THE SHOP...IT BECAME CLEAR THE ELVES WERE MAKING MORE TOYS...AND BETTER THAN EVER!!!!
FRANKLY, I FEEL EMPOWERED.... IN FACT... I'VE BECOME MORE OF A CONCEPTUAL-LEVEL ELF ... AND I HAVE THREE ELVES WORKING WITH ME NOW IN TOY CONSTRUCTION.
AND I... AM ENLIGHTENED (NAMASTE), THROUGH THIS NEW, STRANGE ROCKING-ELF... I MAKE A BETTER TOY, FRANKLY.

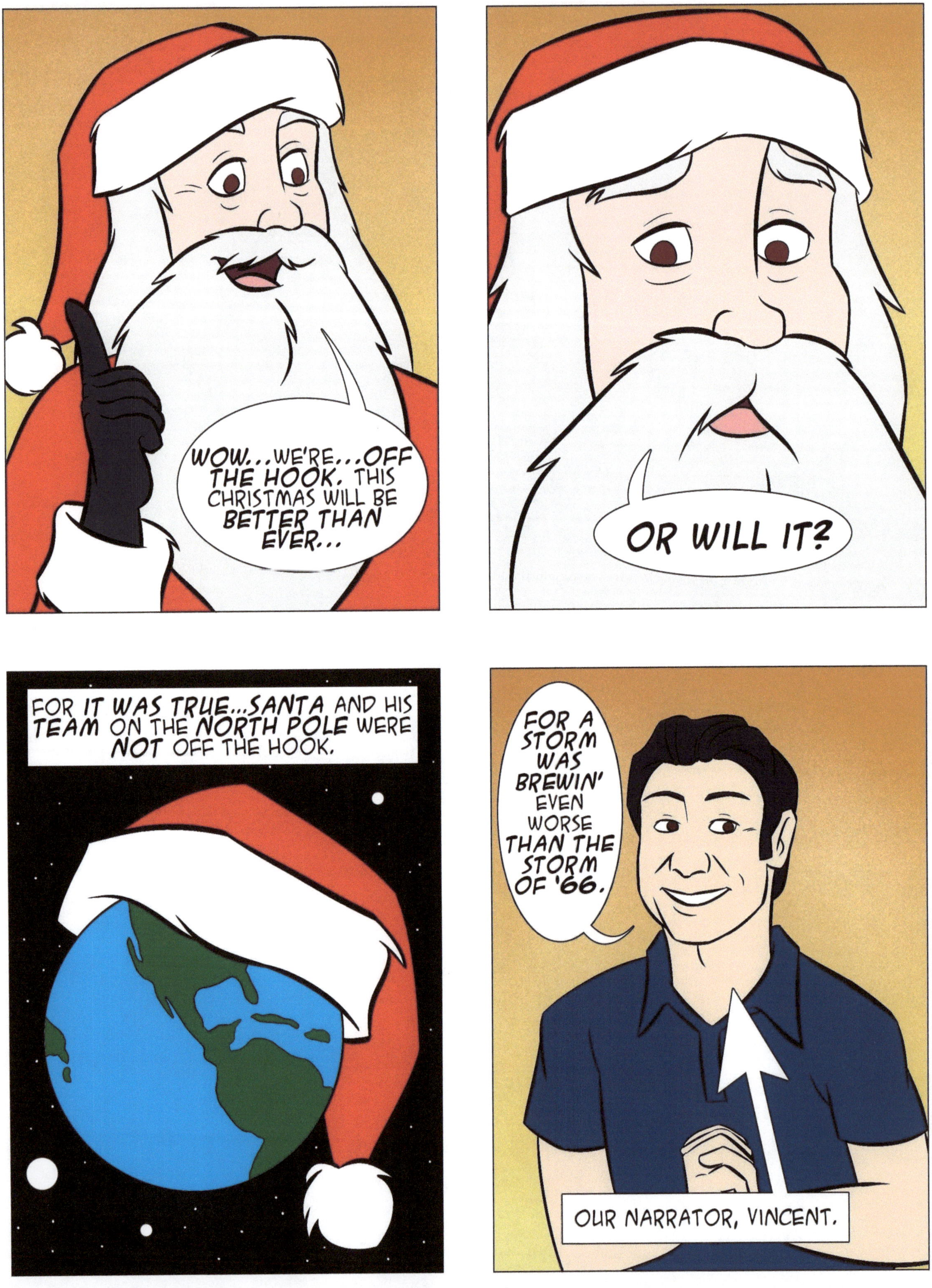
WOW...WE'RE...OFF THE HOOK. THIS CHRISTMAS WILL BE BETTER THAN EVER...
OR WILL IT?
FOR IT WAS TRUE...SANTA AND HIS TEAM ON THE NORTH POLE WERE NOT OFF THE HOOK.
FOR A STORM WAS BREWIN' EVEN WORSE THAN THE STORM OF '66.
OUR NARRATOR, VINCENT.

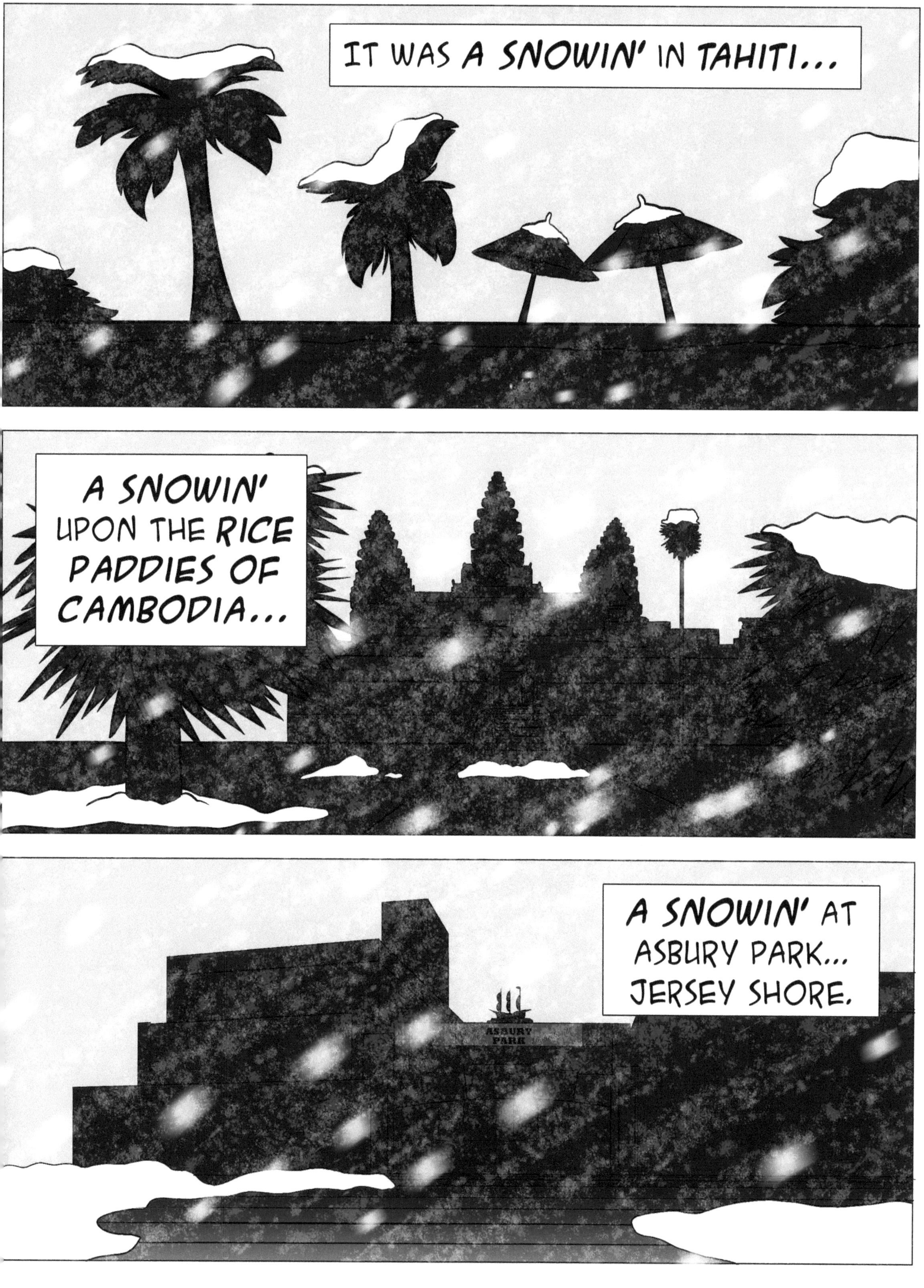
IT WAS A SNOWIN' IN TAHITI...
A SNOWIN' UPON THE RICE PADDIES OF CAMBODIA...
ASBURY PARK
A SNOWIN' AT ASBURY PARK... JERSEY SHORE.

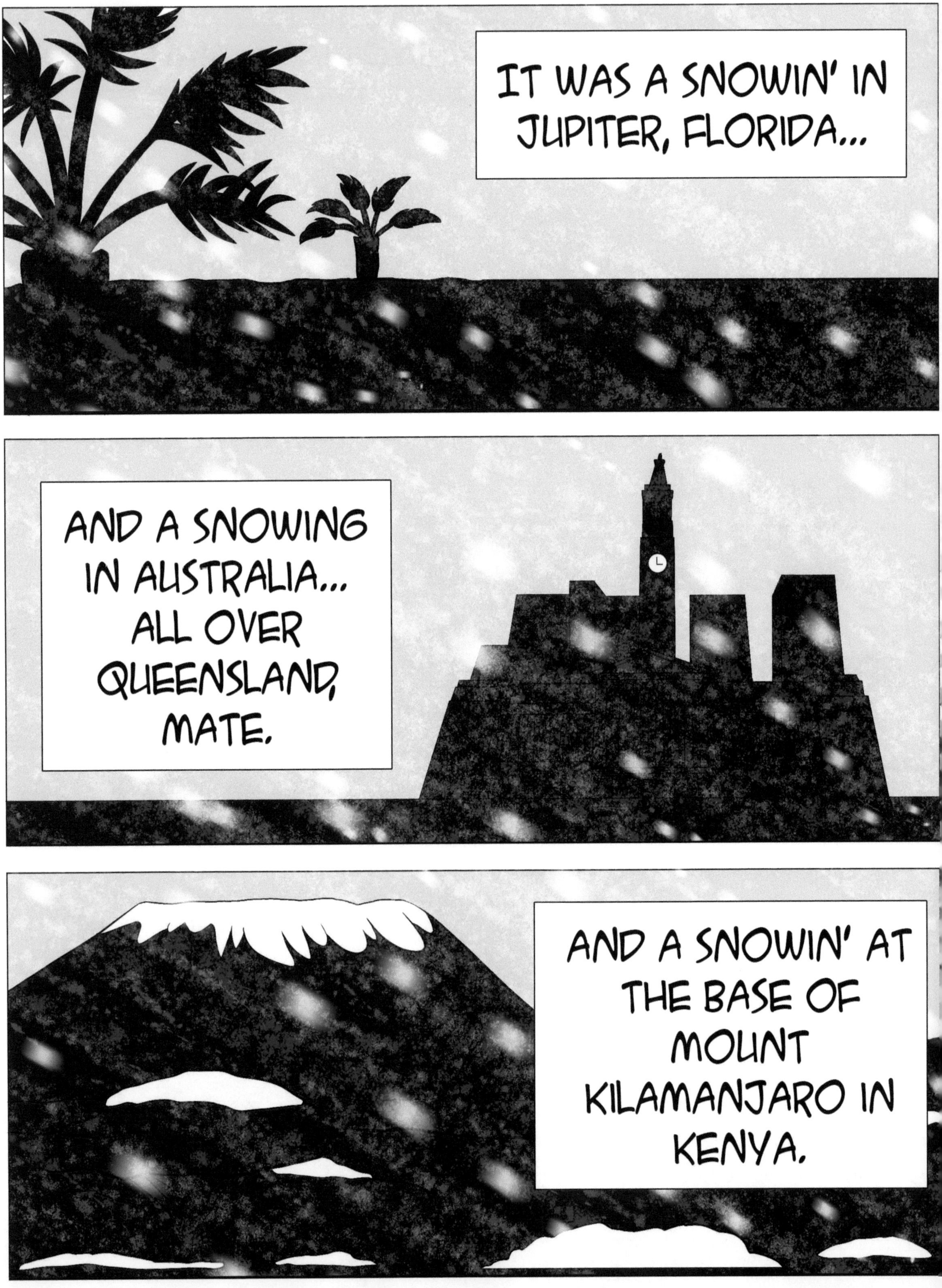
IT WAS A SNOWIN' IN JUPITER, FLORIDA...
AND A SNOWING IN AUSTRALIA... ALL OVER QUEENSLAND, MATE.
AND A SNOWIN' AT THE BASE OF MOUNT KILAMANJARO IN KENYA.

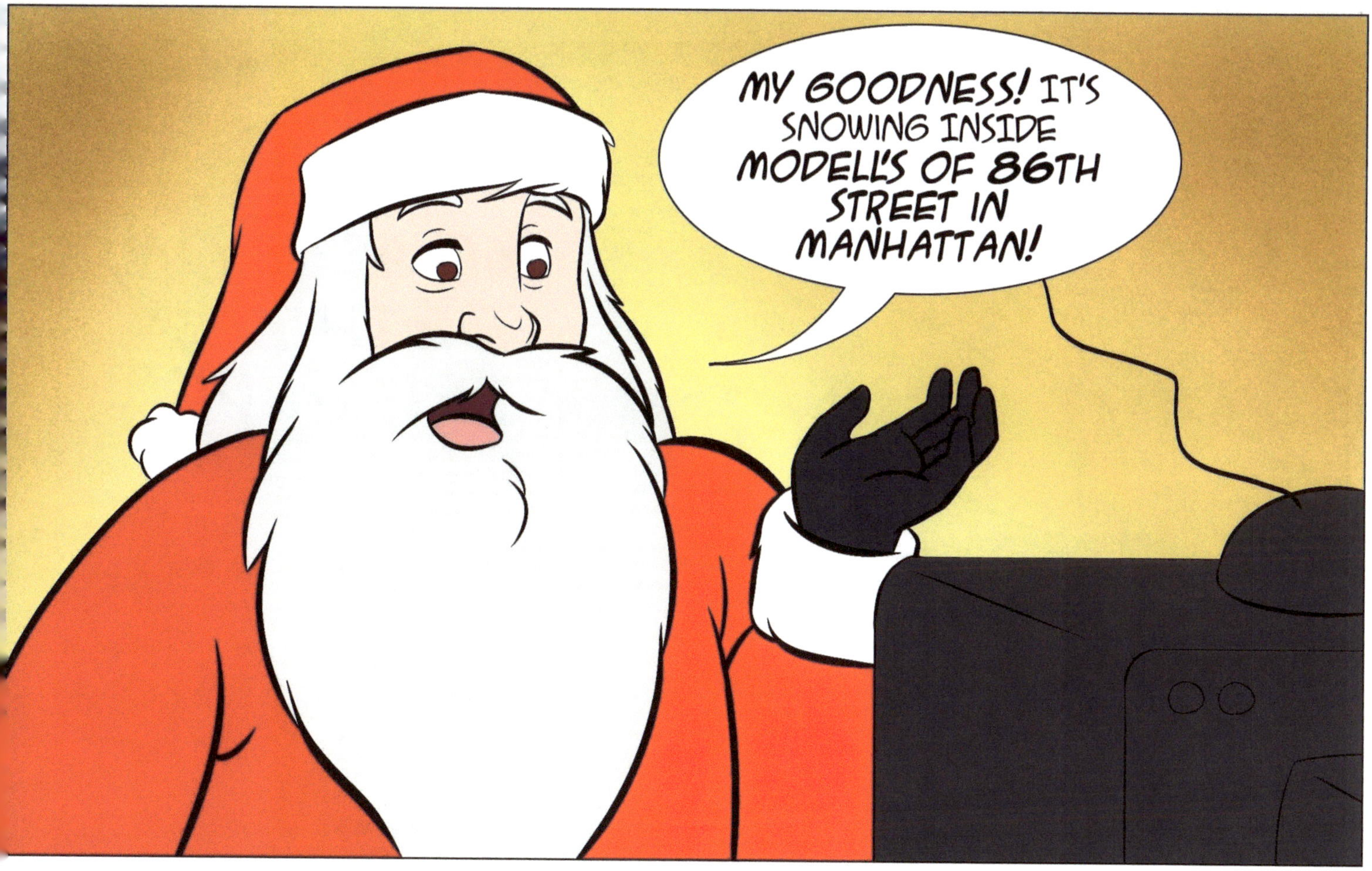
MY GOODNESS! IT'S SNOWING INSIDE MODELL'S OF 86TH STREET IN MANHATTAN!

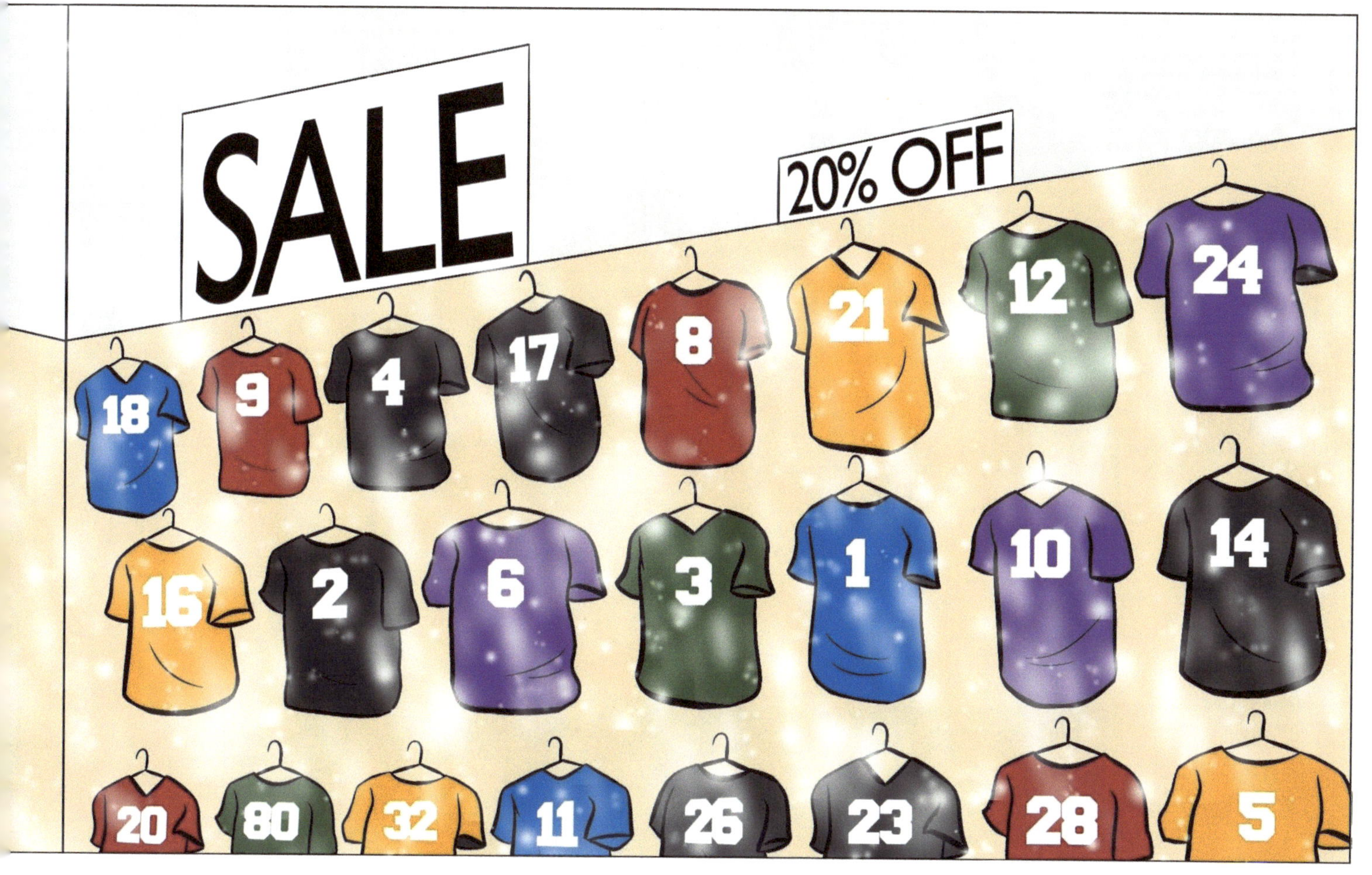
SALE
20% OFF
18
9
4
17
8
21
12
24
16
2
6
3
1
10
14
20
80
32
11
26
23
28
5

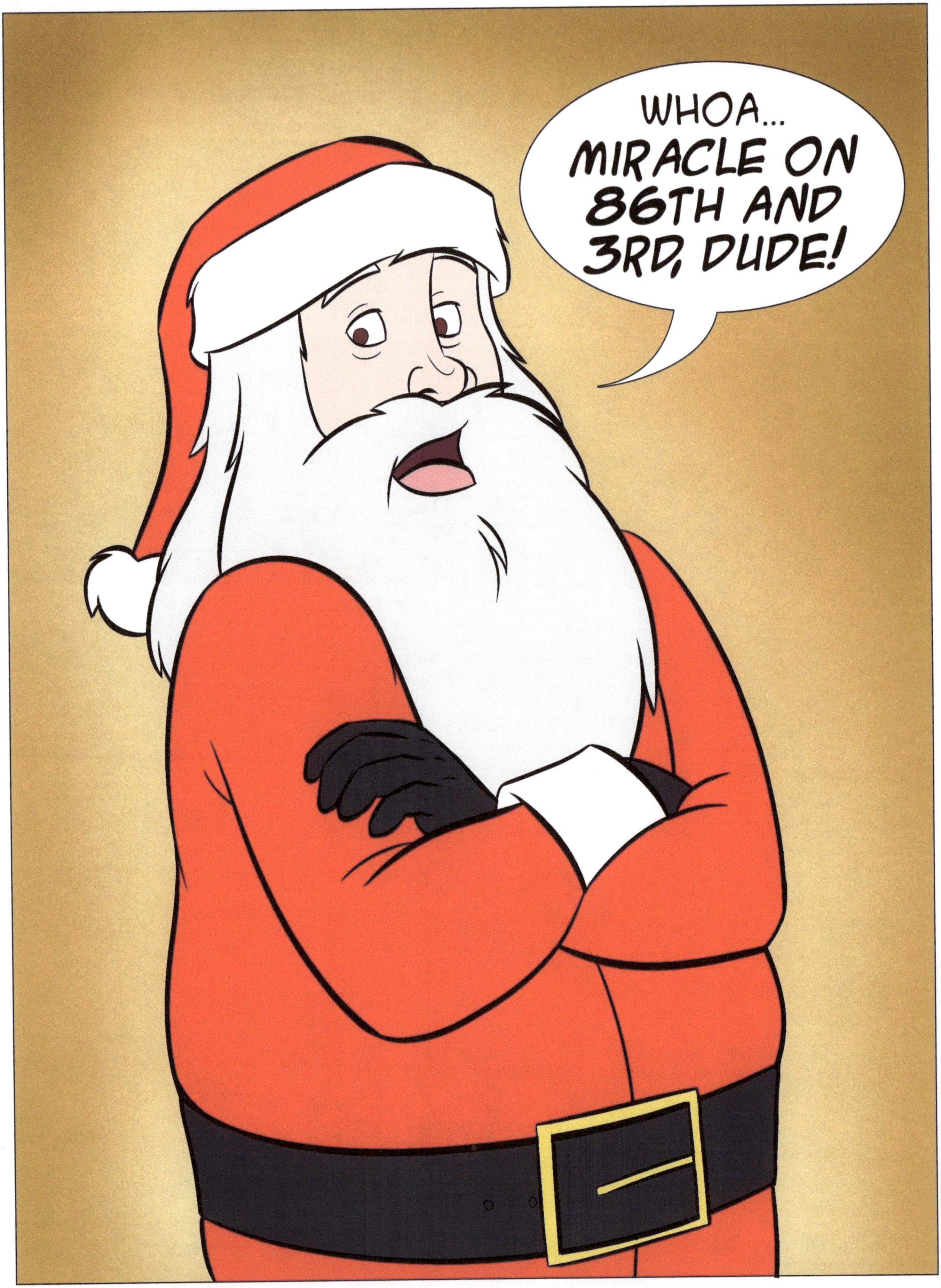
WHOA... MIRACLE ON 86TH AND 3RD, DUDE!

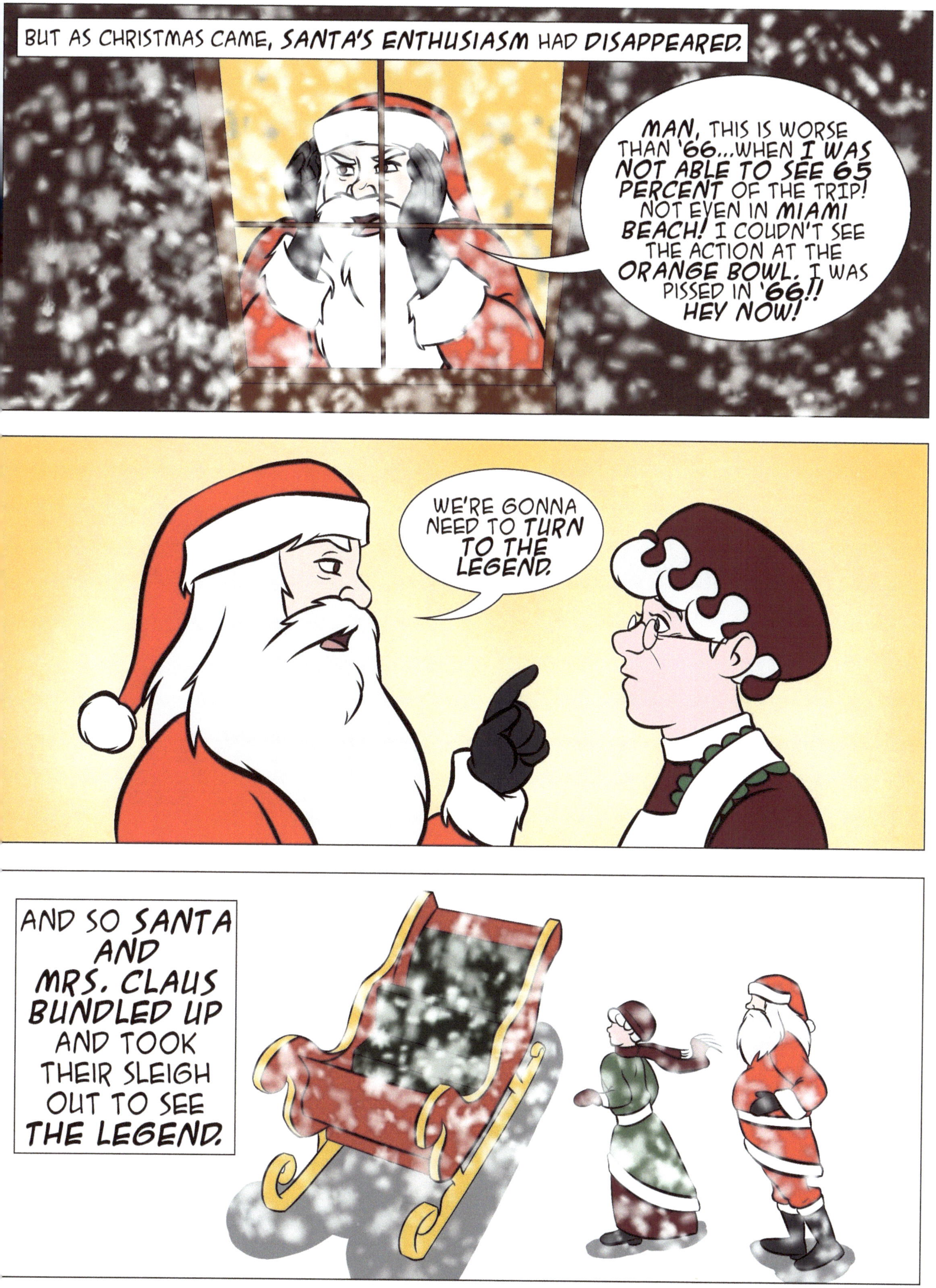
BUT AS CHRISTMAS CAME, SANTA'S ENTHUSIASM HAD DISAPPEARED.
MAN, THIS IS WORSE THAN '66...WHEN I WAS NOT ABLE TO SEE 65 PERCENT OF THE TRIP! NOT EVEN IN MIAMI BEACH! I COUDN'T SEE THE ACTION AT THE ORANGE BOWL. I WAS PISSED IN '66!! HEY NOW!
WE'RE GONNA NEED TO TURN TO THE LEGEND.
AND SO SANTA AND MRS. CLAUS BUNDLED UP AND TOOK THEIR SLEIGH OUT TO SEE THE LEGEND.

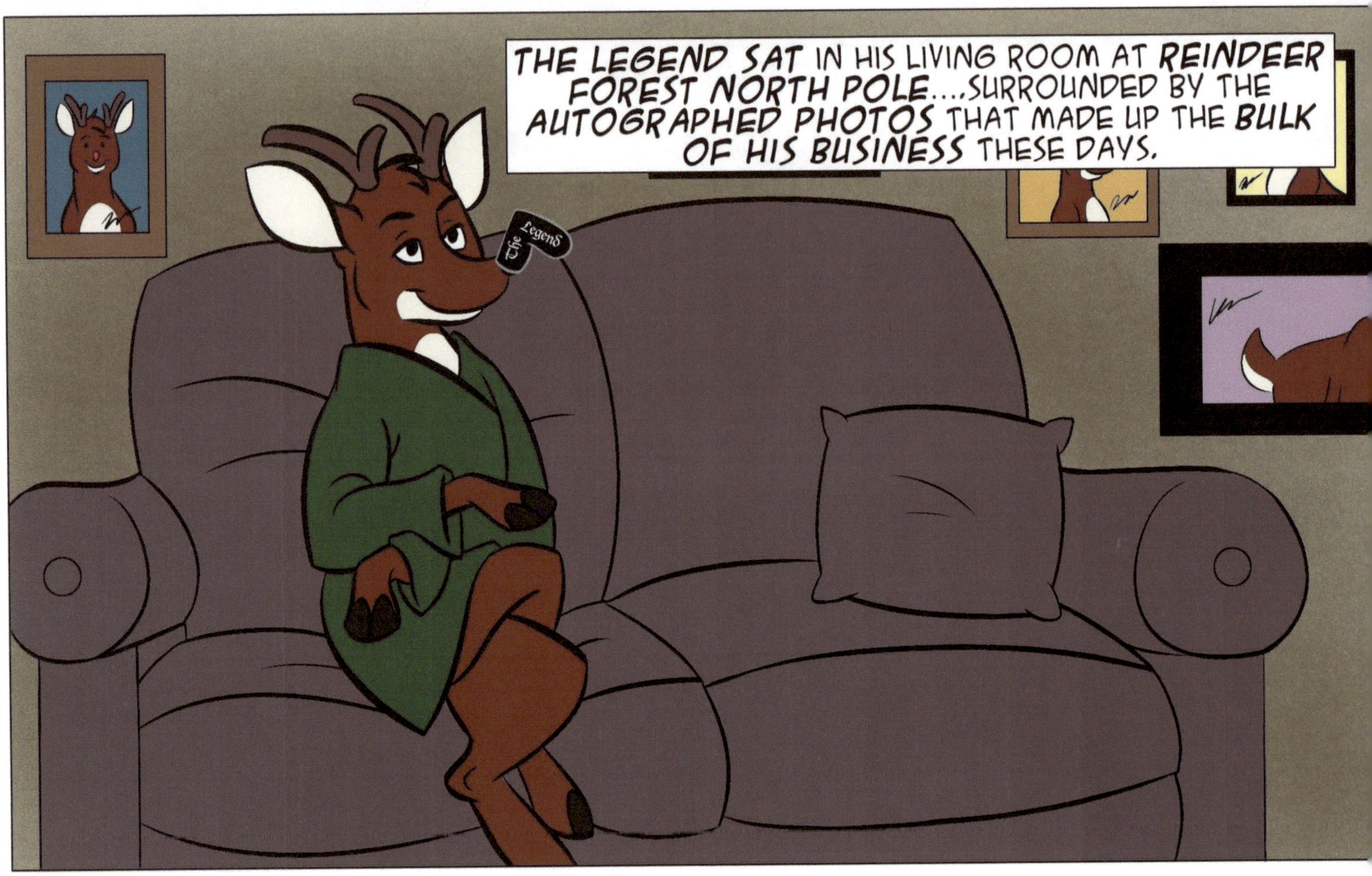
THE LEGEND SAT IN HIS LIVING ROOM AT REINDEER FOREST NORTH POLE....SURROUNDED BY THE AUTOGRAPHED PHOTOS THAT MADE UP THE BULK OF HIS BUSINESS THESE DAYS.
The Legend

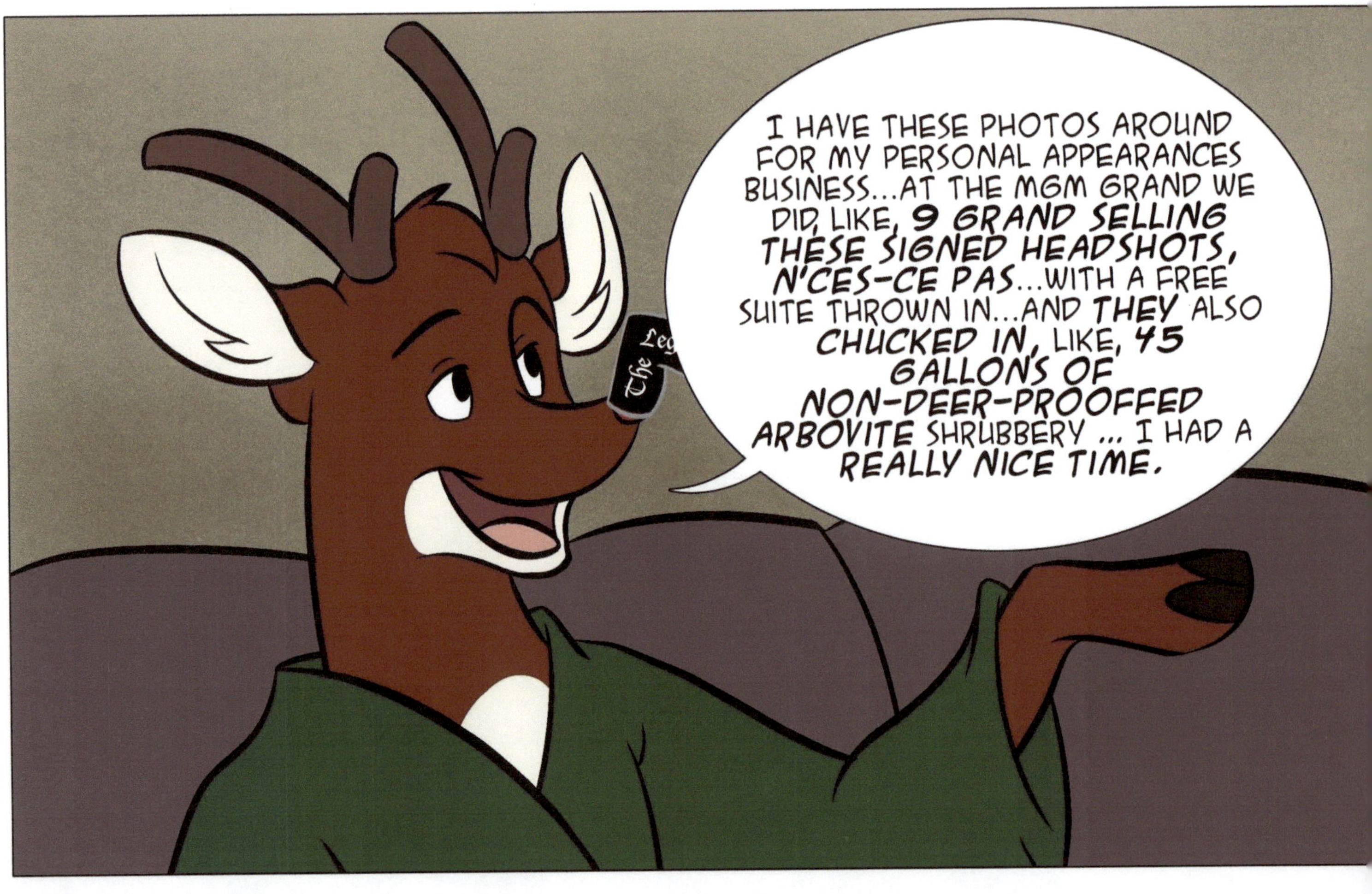
The Leg
I HAVE THESE PHOTOS AROUND FOR MY PERSONAL APPEARANCES BUSINESS...AT THE MGM GRAND WE DID, LIKE, 9 GRAND SELLING THESE SIGNED HEADSHOTS, N'CES-CE PAS...WITH A FREE SUITE THROWN IN...AND THEY ALSO CHUCKED IN, LIKE, 45 GALLON'S OF NON-DEER-PROOFFED ARBOVITE SHRUBBERY ... I HAD A REALLY NICE TIME.

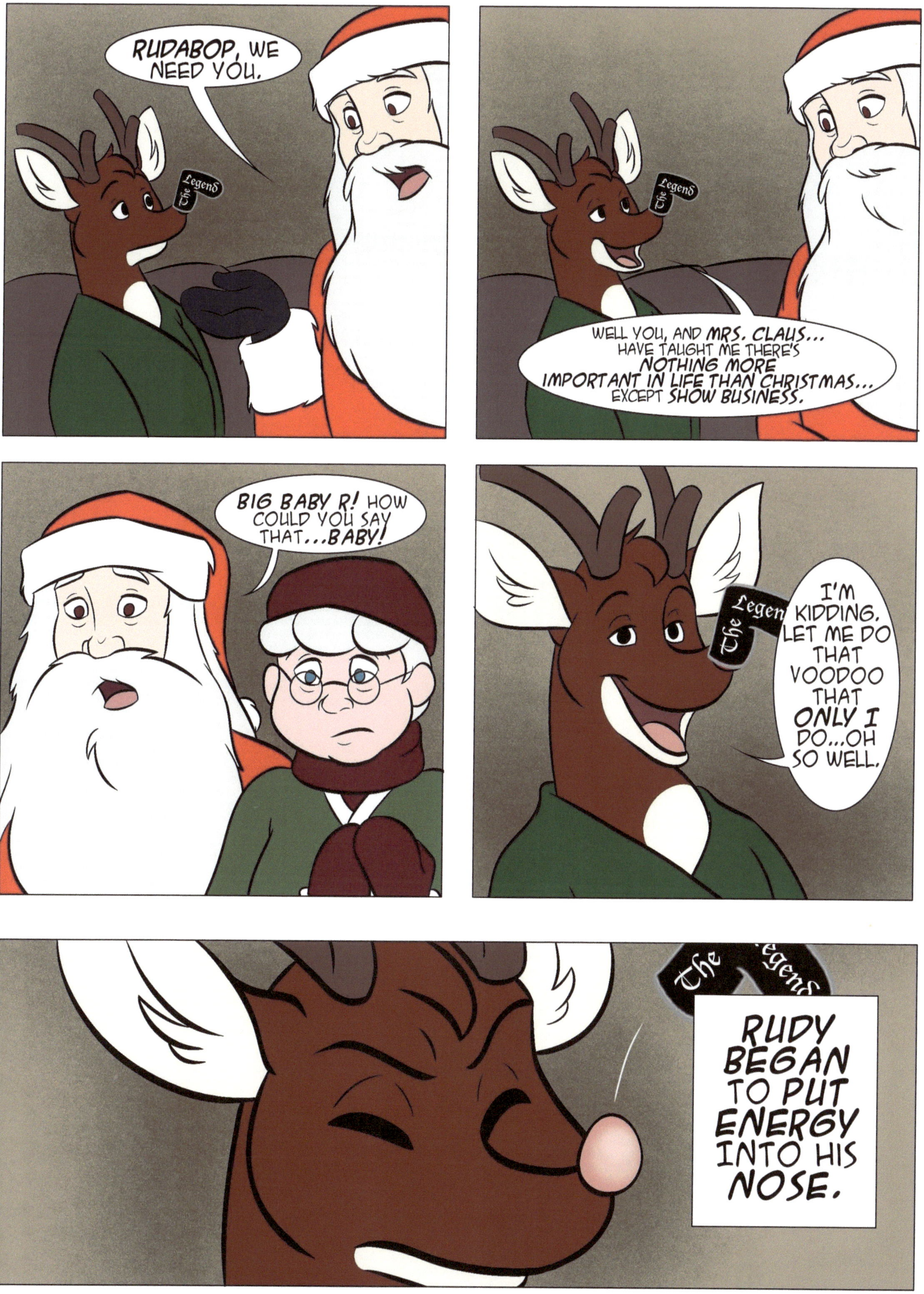
RUDABOP, WE NEED YOU.
The Legend
WELL YOU, AND MRS. CLAUS... HAVE TAUGHT ME THERE'S NOTHING MORE IMPORTANT IN LIFE THAN CHRISTMAS... EXCEPT SHOW BUSINESS.
BIG BABY R! HOW COULD YOU SAY THAT...BABY!
I'M KIDDING. LET ME DO THAT VOODOO THAT ONLY I DO...OH SO WELL.
RUDY BEGAN TO PUT ENERGY INTO HIS NOSE.

WAIT A MINUTE... THERE'S NOTHING GOING ON.
MY NOSE ISN'T LIGHTING UP!
YES, IN FACT, THE LEGEND'S NOSE STARTED TURNING VIOLET.
JIMINY CRICKEY!
AND THEN IT WENT OUT ALL TOGETHER...
IF THIS MEANS WE HAVE TO CALL TIME WARNER CABLE... I'M THROWING UP.

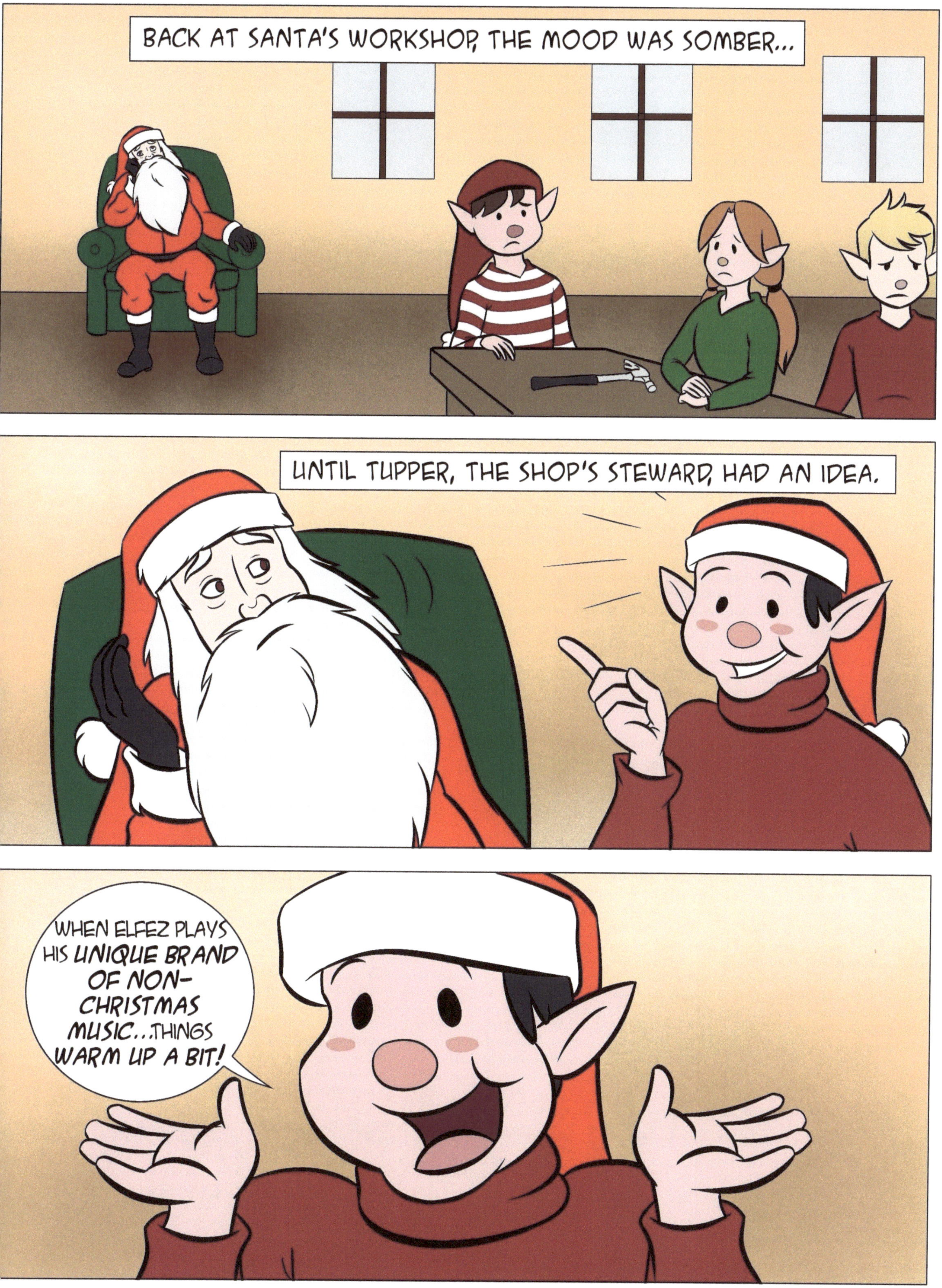
BACK AT SANTA'S WORKSHOP, THE MOOD WAS SOMBER...
UNTIL TUPPER, THE SHOP'S STEWARD, HAD AN IDEA.
WHEN ELFEZ PLAYS HIS UNIQUE BRAND OF NON-CHRISTMAS MUSIC...THINGS WARM UP A BIT!

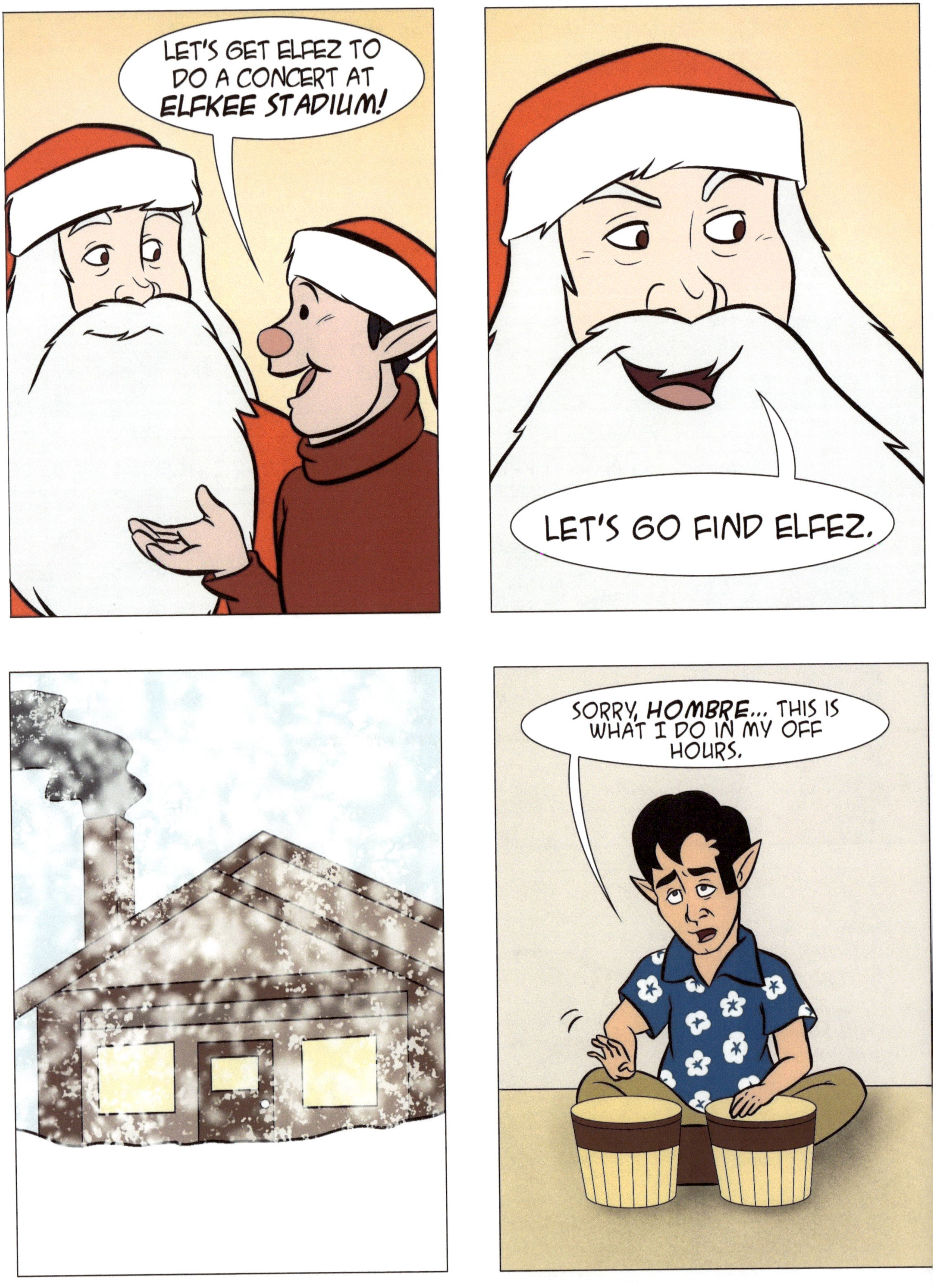
LET'S GET ELFEZ TO DO A CONCERT AT ELFKEE STADIUM!
LET'S GO FIND ELFEZ.
SORRY, HOMBRE... THIS IS WHAT I DO IN MY OFF HOURS.

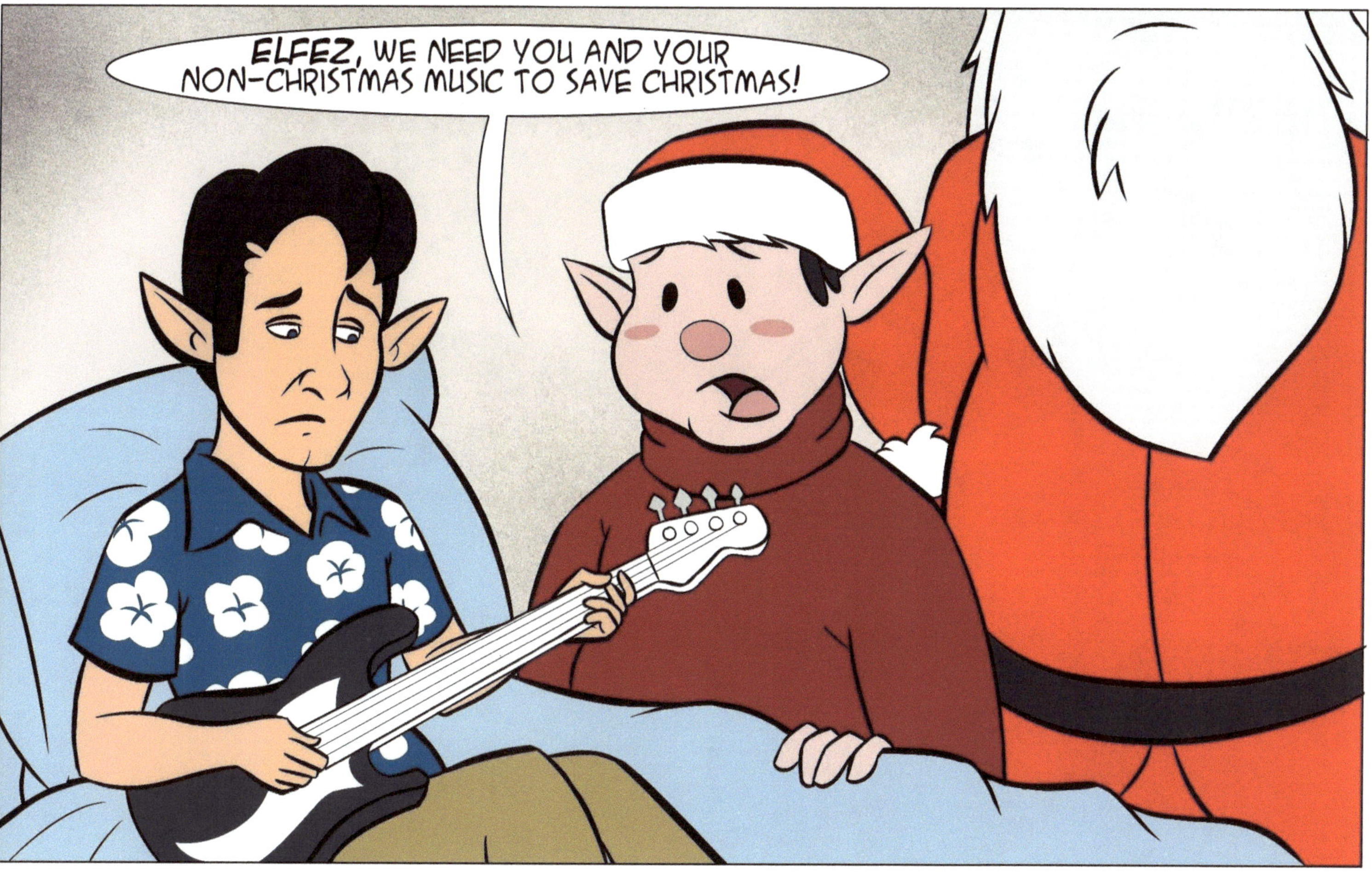
ELFEZ, WE NEED YOU AND YOUR NON-CHRISTMAS MUSIC TO SAVE CHRISTMAS!

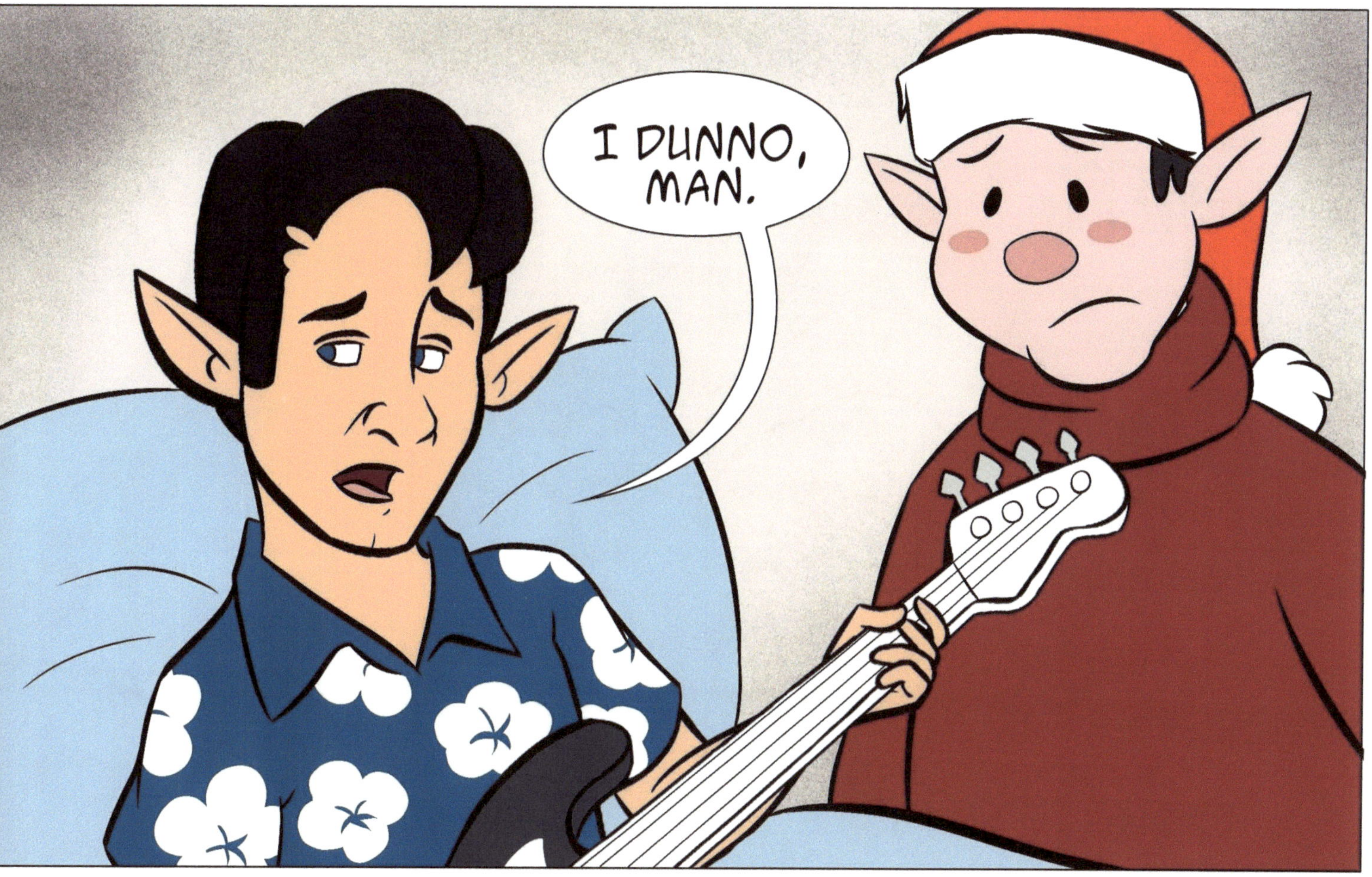
I DUNNO, MAN.

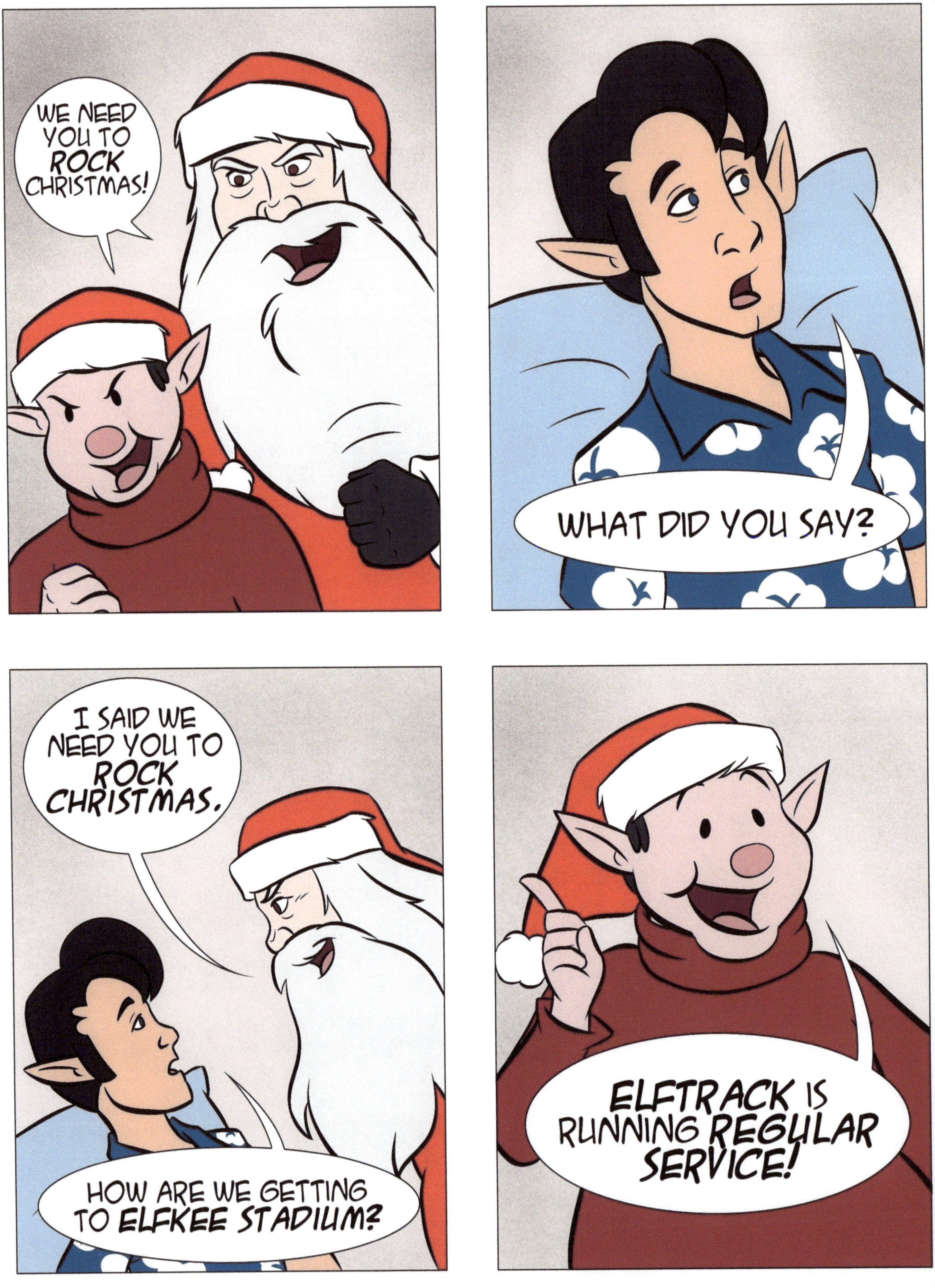
WE NEED YOU TO ROCK CHRISTMAS!
WHAT DID YOU SAY?
I SAID WE NEED YOU TO ROCK CHRISTMAS.
HOW ARE WE GETTING TO ELFKEE STADIUM?
ELFTRACK IS RUNNING REGULAR SERVICE!

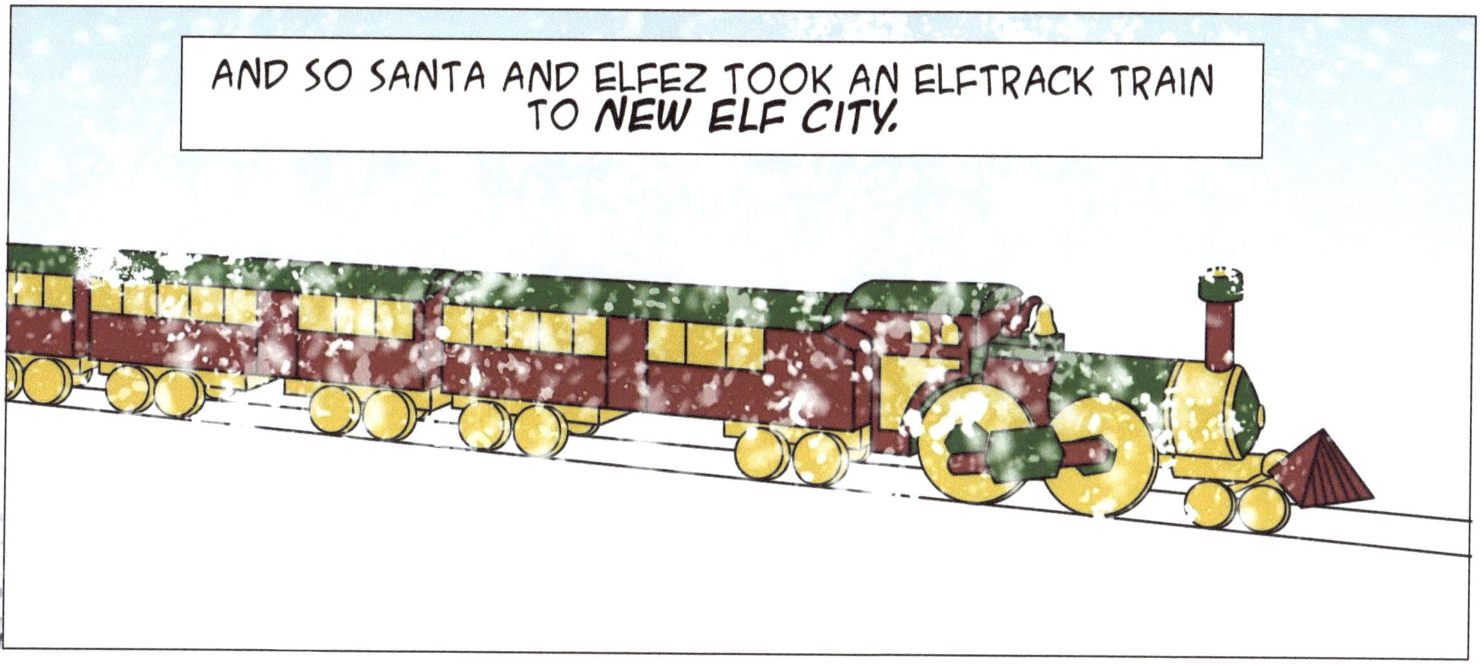
AND SO SANTA AND ELFEZ TOOK AN ELFTRACK TRAIN TO NEW ELF CITY.

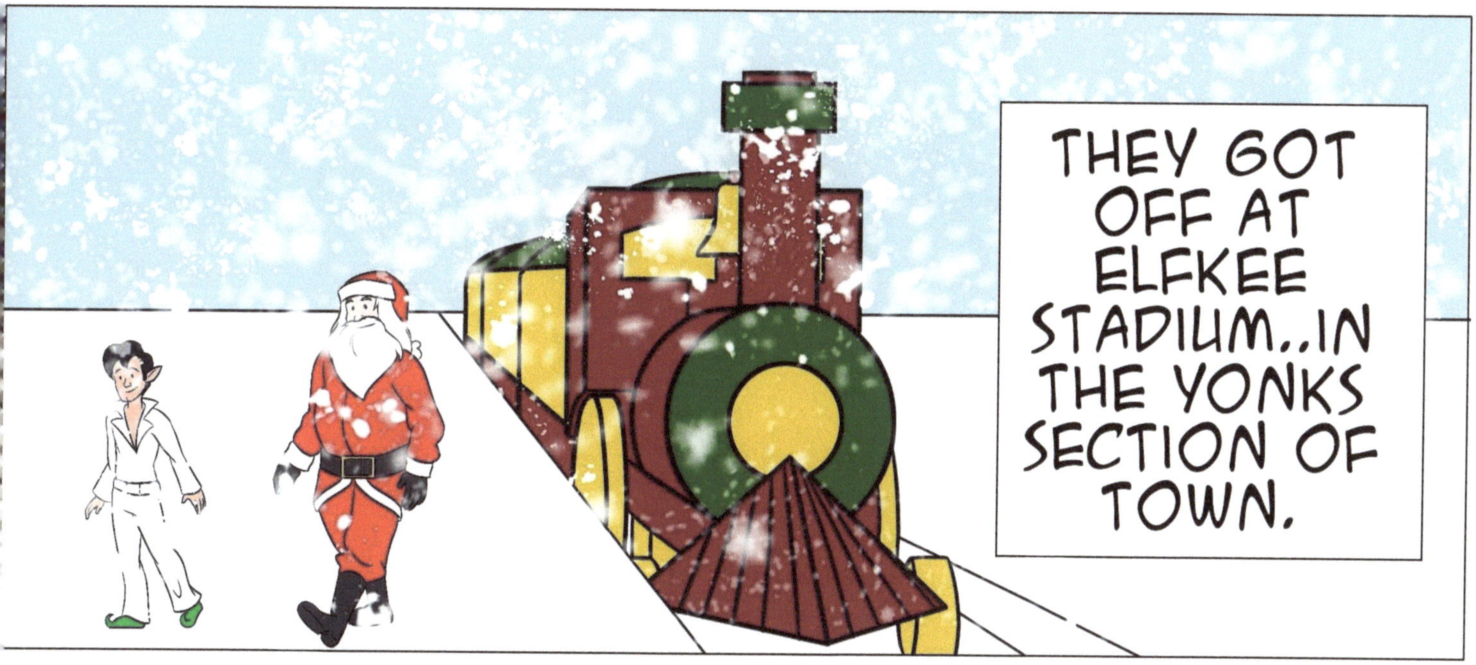
THEY GOT OFF AT ELFKEE STADIUM..IN THE YONKS SECTION OF TOWN.

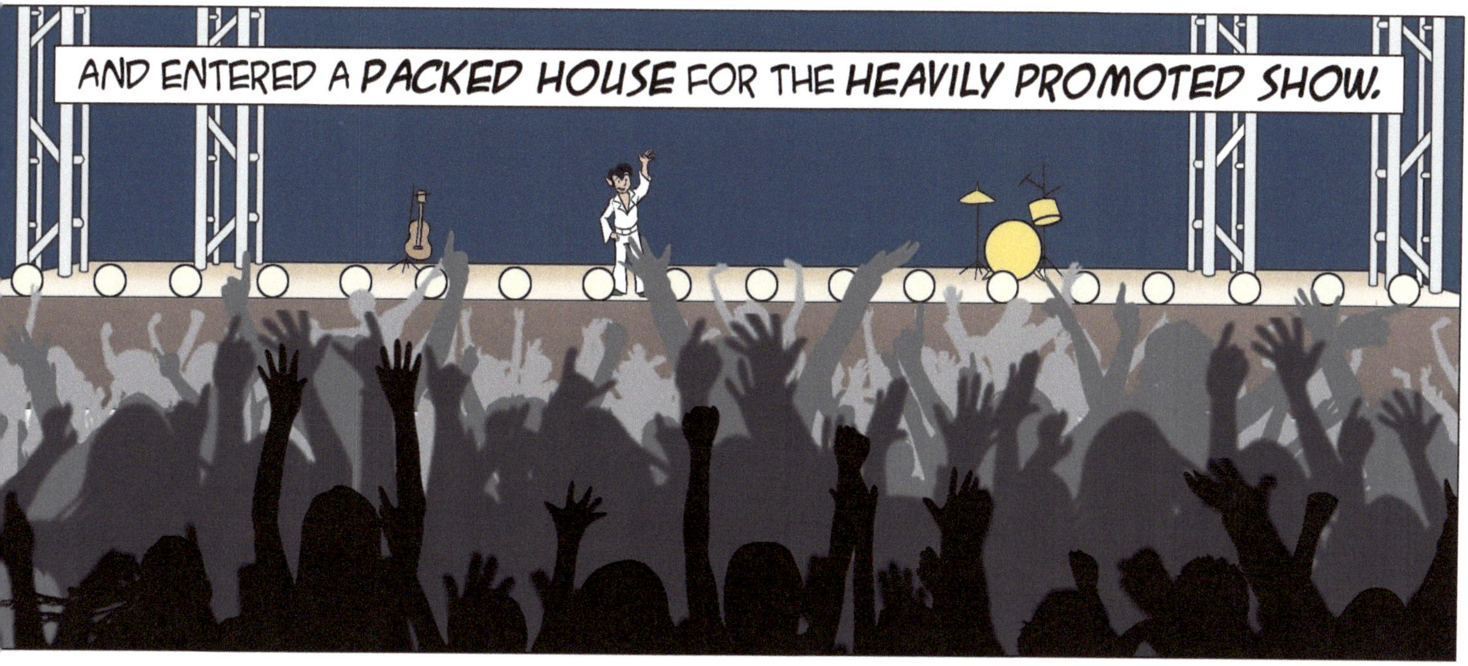
AND ENTERED A PACKED HOUSE FOR THE HEAVILY PROMOTED SHOW.

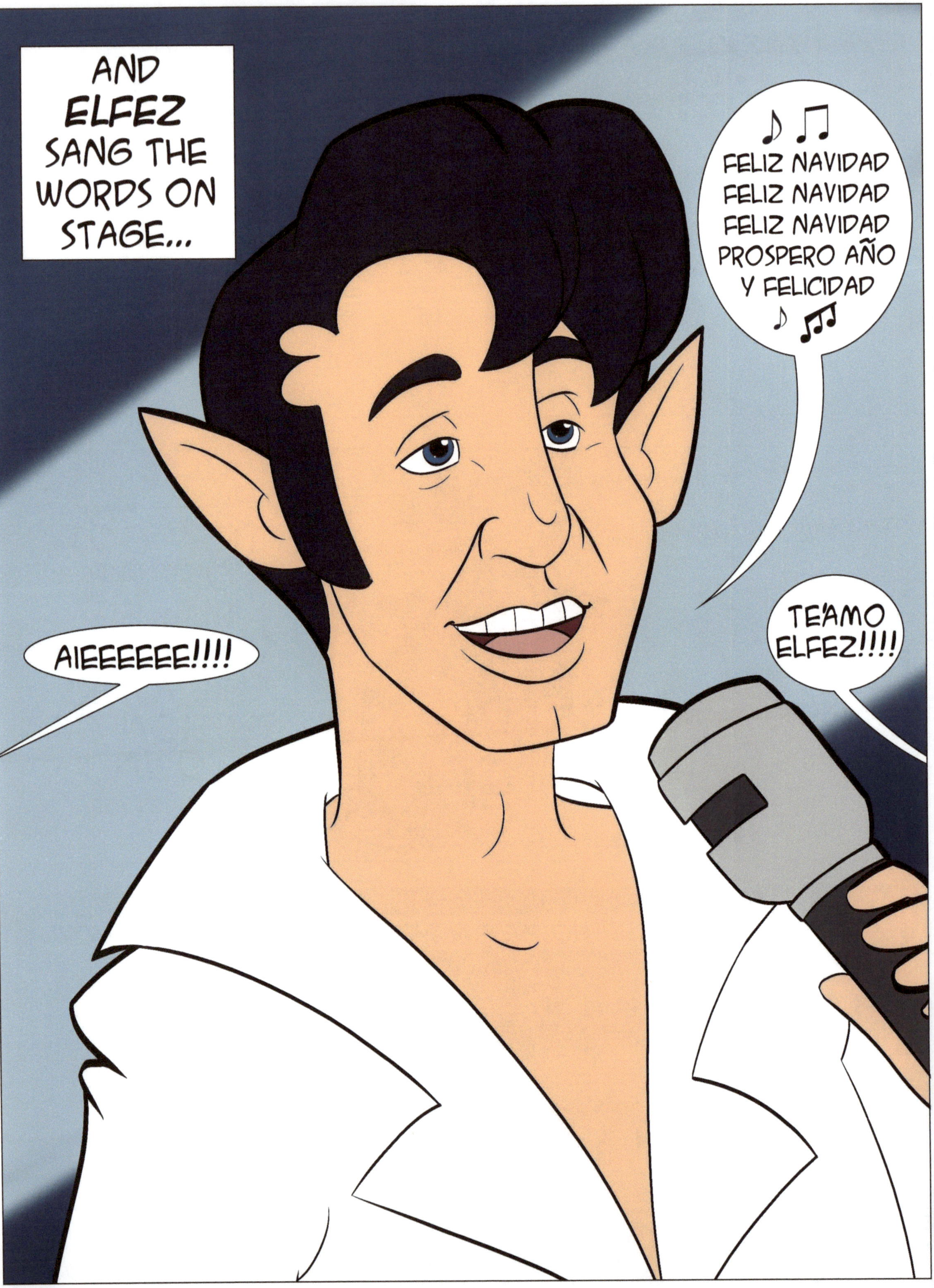
AND ELFEZ SANG THE WORDS ON STAGE...
♪ ♫ FELIZ NAVIDAD FELIZ NAVIDAD FELIZ NAVIDAD PROSPERO AÑO Y FELICIDAD ♪ ♫
AIEEEEEEE!!!!
TE'AMO ELFEZ!!!!

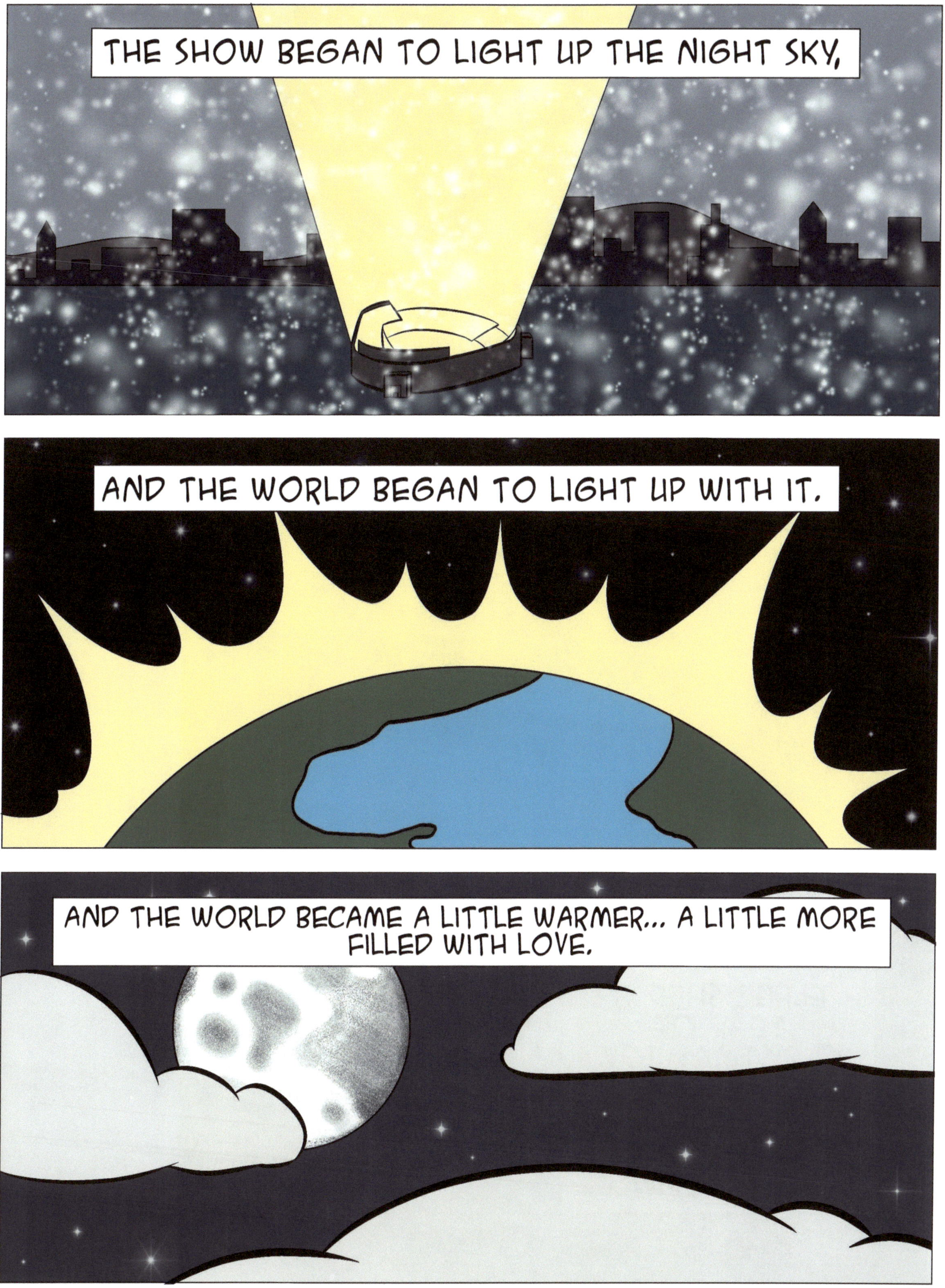
THE SHOW BEGAN TO LIGHT UP THE NIGHT SKY,
AND THE WORLD BEGAN TO LIGHT UP WITH IT.
AND THE WORLD BECAME A LITTLE WARMER... A LITTLE MORE FILLED WITH LOVE.

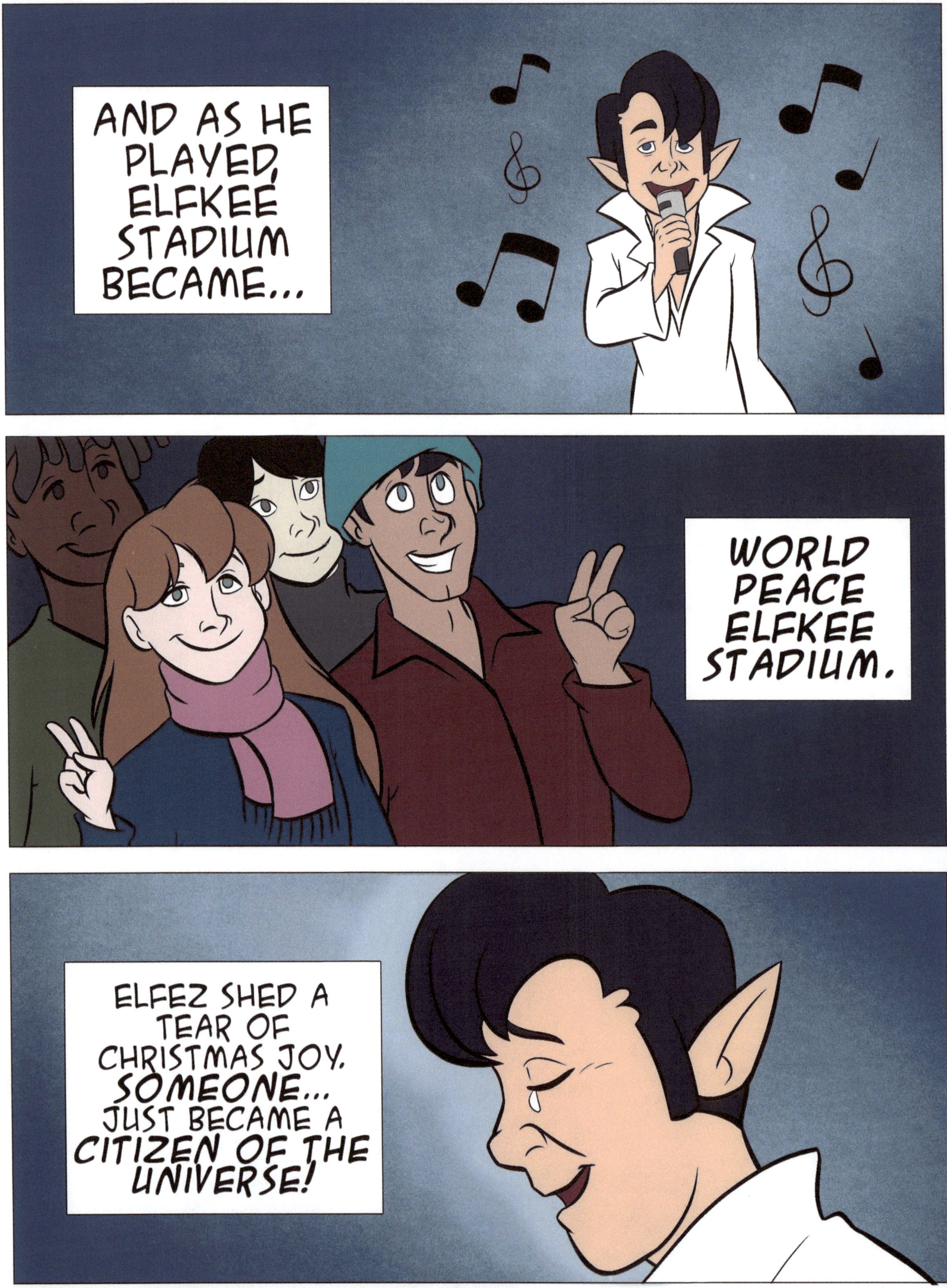
AND AS HE PLAYED, ELFKEE STADIUM BECAME...
WORLD PEACE ELFKEE STADIUM.
ELFEZ SHED A TEAR OF CHRISTMAS JOY. SOMEONE... JUST BECAME A CITIZEN OF THE UNIVERSE!

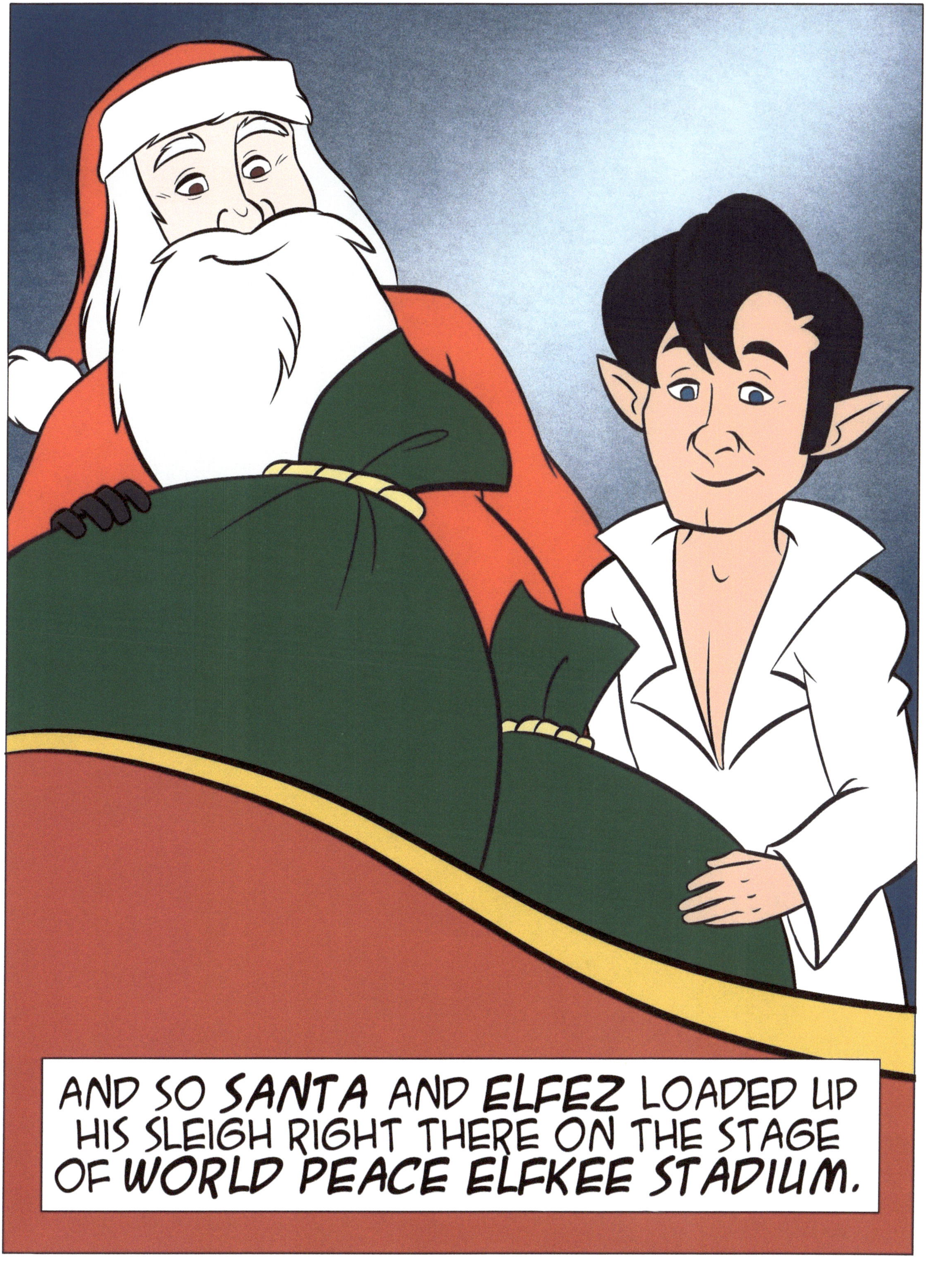
AND SO SANTA AND ELFEZ LOADED UP HIS SLEIGH RIGHT THERE ON THE STAGE OF WORLD PEACE ELFKEE STADIUM.

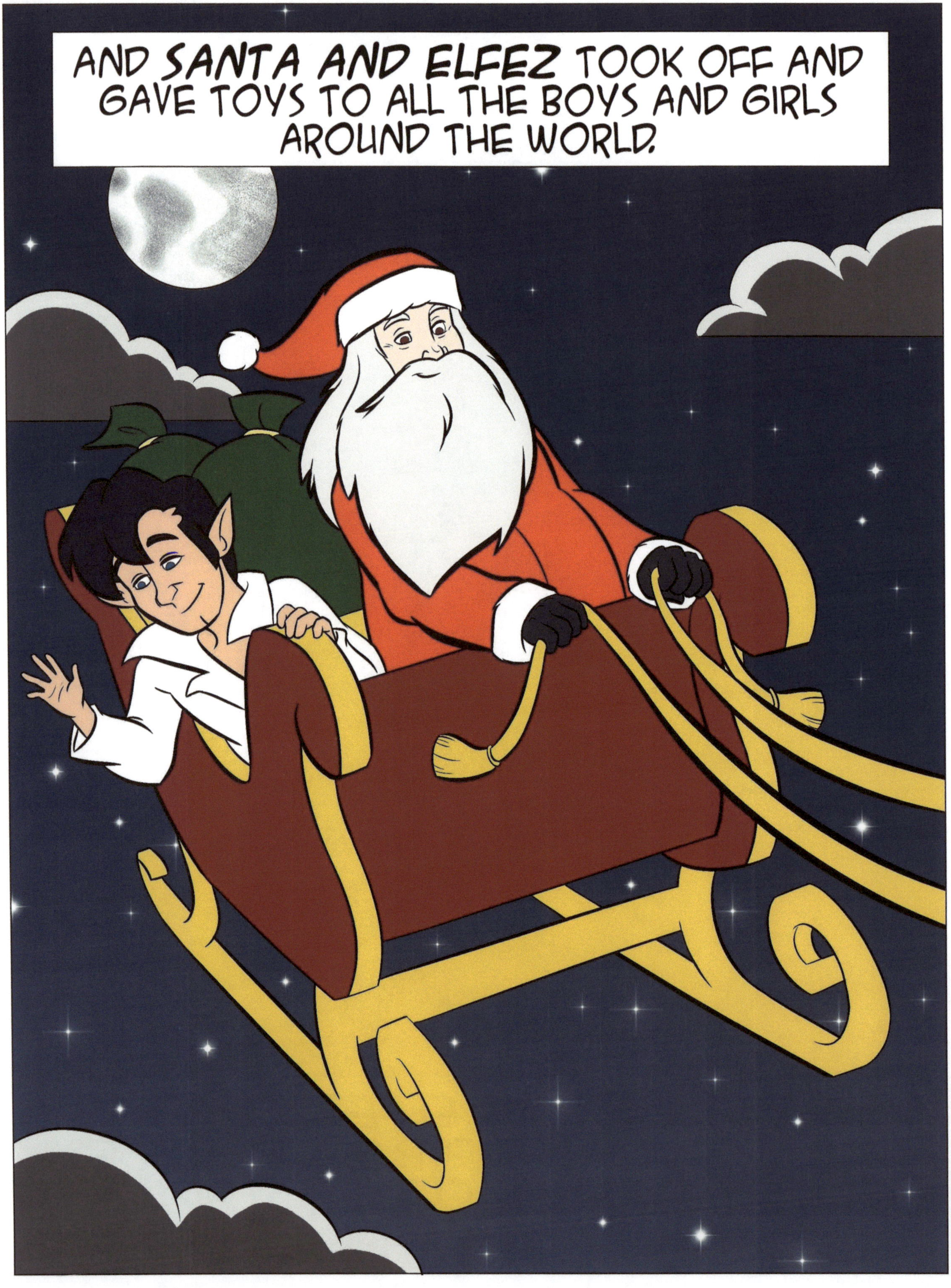
AND SANTA AND ELFEZ TOOK OFF AND GAVE TOYS TO ALL THE BOYS AND GIRLS AROUND THE WORLD.

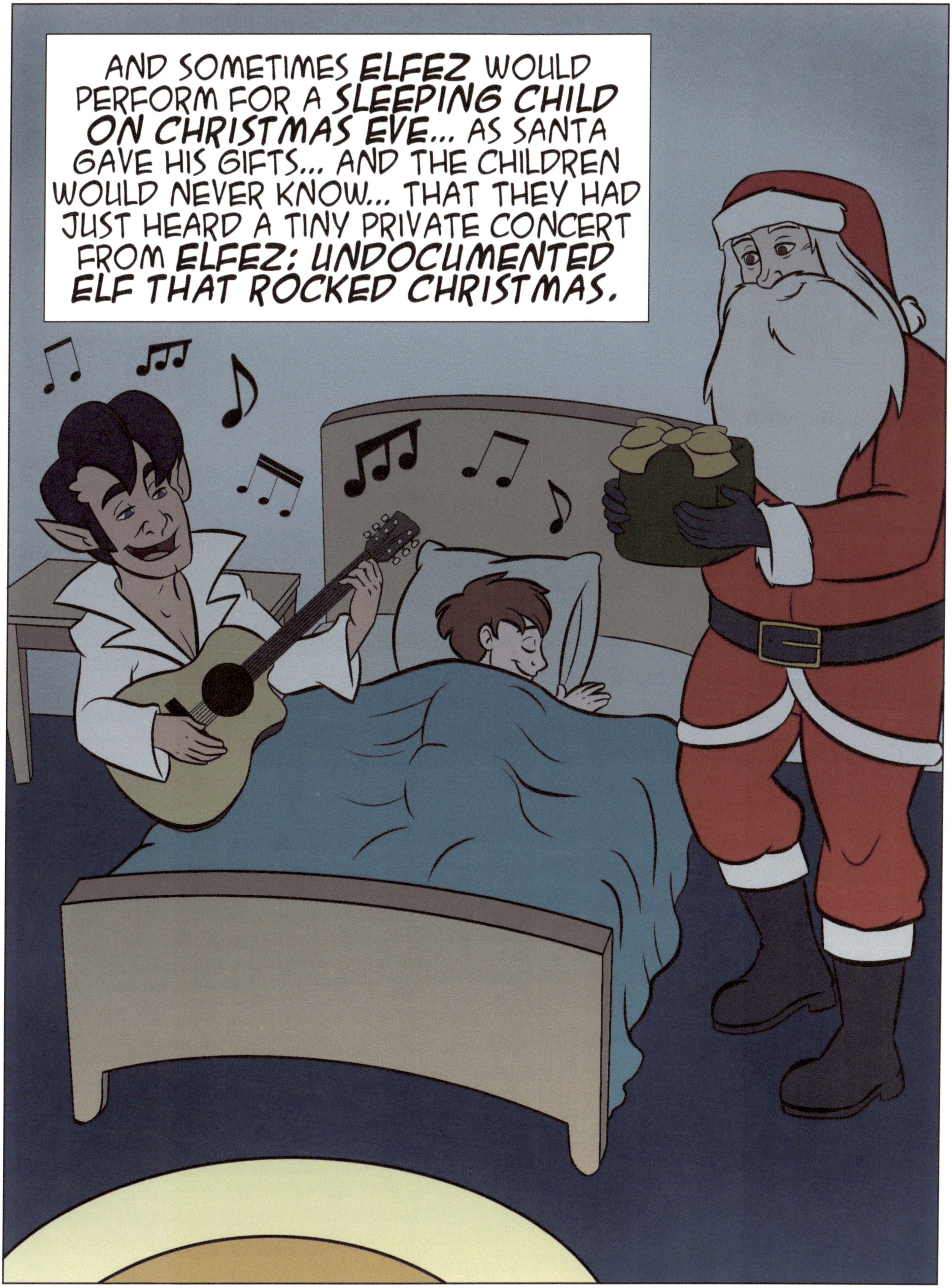
AND SOMETIMES ELFEZ WOULD PERFORM FOR A SLEEPING CHILD ON CHRISTMAS EVE... AS SANTA GAVE HIS GIFTS... AND THE CHILDREN WOULD NEVER KNOW... THAT THEY HAD JUST HEARD A TINY PRIVATE CONCERT FROM ELFEZ: UNDOCUMENTED ELF THAT ROCKED CHRISTMAS.

www.ingramcontent.com/pod-product-compliance
Lightning Source LLC
Chambersburg PA
CBHW042130040426
42450CB00003B/140
*9780692970959*